OPPORTUNITIES

in

Overseas
Careers

D0167424

OPPORTUNITIES

in

Overseas
Careers

REVISED EDITION

BLYTHE CAMENSON

VGM Career Books

New York   Chicago   San Francisco   Lisbon   London   Madrid   Mexico City
Milan   New Delhi   San Juan   Seoul   Singapore   Sydney   Toronto

The *McGraw-Hill* Companies

Library of Congress Cataloging-in-Publication Data

Camenson, Blythe.
  Opportunities in overseas careers / Blythe Camenson.— Rev. ed.
      p.   cm. — (VGM opportunities series)
    ISBN 0-07-143725-8
    1. Americans—Employment—Foreign countries.   2. Vocational guidance.
  I. Title.   II. Series.

  HF5549.5.E45C32   2004
  331.702—dc22   2004006070

1 2 3 4 5 6 7 8 9 0   DOC/DOC   3 2 1 0 9 8 7 6 5 4

ISBN 0-07-143725-8

Interior design by Rattray Design

McGraw-Hill books are available at special quantity discounts to use as premiums and sales promotions, or for use in corporate training programs. For more information, please write to the Director of Special Sales, Professional Publishing, McGraw-Hill, Two Penn Plaza, New York, NY 10121-2298. Or contact your local bookstore.

This book is printed on acid-free paper.

To all my expatriate friends around the world
who made my time overseas so enjoyable.

Contents

What it's like living and working overseas. Who's hiring. Overseas salaries and other perks. What does it all add up to?

Job-hunting avenues. Adding to your skills bank.

Subcontracting. Types of jobs. Salary and benefits. What the work is like. Recreation. Culture. Advice.

Foreword

Why leave the safety and security of your home country, your own backyard, to face the uncertainties of life overseas? Many do it simply for the money. Others cite the value of international experience and enhanced résumé to their career. I believe the pleasures and challenges posed by a new culture represent the best reasons. However, there's no right or wrong reason to live and work abroad.

For some, the desire to spread their wings and explore new horizons is satisfied by a vacation in a foreign land. For others, this craving might be fulfilled by a year working and traveling, as a volunteer in Latin America perhaps, or as a teacher of English in the Far East. Working abroad on a more permanent basis, however, offers the greatest challenge—and the greatest benefits: total immersion in a new country and culture is a rich experience that is comparable to few others. It enables those lucky enough to do so to get an entirely different perspective, to get beneath the skin of a new culture, to see things as a native rather than as a tourist.

The opportunities to live and work abroad in today's shrinking world are numerous, and they are restricted only by the imagination. The liberalized global economy, dominated as it is by multinational business activity, offers greater and more varied opportunities than ever before, and there is every sign that the opportunities will continue to grow and expand well into the next century.

Who can work abroad? Where are the opportunities? The demand for imported expertise in Africa and Latin America all stimulate a high volume of employment opportunities for those foreigners who possess technical and commercial skills.

The booming economies of the Far East mean there are funds galore for new hospitals, power plants, telecommunications systems, ports, and transportation—particularly new highways and airports.

To sustain growth and output, there is particular need for skilled professionals such as engineers and other construction specialists, teachers, medical personnel, and so forth.

It is anticipated that the Far East and the Middle East alone will continue to provide opportunities for qualified Westerners for decades to come. In Europe, too—in spite of high unemployment—there are opportunities for those who are prepared to compete and who want to experience life on the continent.

Those who will find it easiest to find a job abroad are those with the skills, qualifications, and experiences that make them assets in the eyes of foreign employers, particularly in "hot" industries such as information technology and telecommunications.

So you don't need to be a rocket scientist to work abroad; imagination and motivation alone will take you a long way. There are countless opportunities in every industry: education, medicine, science and technology, commerce, agriculture, aviation, and tourism all offer openings to the global job seeker.

At the other end of the scale there are young people who are prepared to take off and live by their wits, accept any job that comes along, and embrace what fate dishes out. The frontiers may have changed, but today's young adventurers, who have replaced the previous generation of free-spirited "flower children," may still be "seeking themselves" and looking for alternative lifestyles. Nonetheless, many are not just joining aid programs for a couple of years; they are putting down roots and getting real jobs.

Gone are the beads and backpacks. Today's young Westerners are arriving with a shirt, tie, and M.B.A. They want the cultural experience, but they also want the money.

Above all, today's successful international job hunters are open-minded about foreign cultures and adapt quickly to life away from home. They are prepared to learn new skills and new languages, and they accept new and different lifestyles.

While the trend today is moving away from the lavish expatriate packages that were once standard—including fat salaries, bonuses and perks, free home flights, accommodations, car, club membership, and schooling—good deals are still available.

It is timely, then, that this excellent book on the subject is available to help put the international job hunter on the right road.

Daniel James
Assistant Editor
Overseas Jobs Express
West Sussex, England

Acknowledgments

The author would like to thank the following professionals for providing information about their work:

John P. Brokaw—music teacher/assistant principal/high
   school principal, DoDDS
Joanne Burch—EFL teacher, international school
Lisa Eagleson-Roever—senior engineer/design standards
   specialist, private company
Vern Liermann—teaching principal/classroom teacher/
   music specialist/assistant principal, DoDDS
Robert Manzanares—Foreign Service officer
James McMullan—EFL teacher, private company
Steve Negley—computer programmer/analyst, private
   company/government contractor
Shirley Panasuk—Foreign Service nurse
Angela Rekowski—math teacher, Peace Corps volunteer
Jim Van Laningham—Foreign Service officer

1

WORKING OVERSEAS

IF YOU ARE reading this book, you are most likely a special breed of person—adventurous, extremely flexible, and tolerant—and whether motivated by finances or your sense of wanderlust, you are open to new experiences and ready to confront whatever awaits you. The idea of working and living overseas is exciting—and viable.

Part of the attraction of working overseas is never knowing exactly what to expect. You might have done all your research, talked to all the right people, followed all the advice in this book and others, but when you get on that plane and head off for a new job, you can never quite be sure what's going to be waiting for you at the other end.

Each country, each city, each employment setting offers something different to each individual who ventures abroad. Successful and contented overseas workers are prepared for the unexpected and open to the unpredictable. They view each new job as a gift, a challenge, and an adventure.

1

Some new employees, for example, have arrived at their destinations to find that their entry visas are not in order or that no one has been instructed to meet them at the airport. Their housing is not ready yet, or their contracts still have not been translated into English. Problems such as these are not insurmountable, and they are eventually worked out—with a little patience and a king-size sense of humor.

Other employees have arrived to discover that their standard of living has suddenly skyrocketed beyond what they had expected, that their social life has become a whirl of activity, and that their professional skills are being utilized to their fullest.

A tolerant attitude will see you through the bumps and allow you to experience all the benefits of your overseas situation. But it should be pointed out that some bumps are insurmountable for the individual employee. Medical facilities could be inadequate, air and/or noise pollution intolerable, living conditions substandard, working conditions chaotic—all with no hope of improvement. If you've given a place a chance, done what you could to make an unlivable situation livable, but it still isn't working, there's no shame in packing your bags once again and leaving. This doesn't happen very often, but when it does, an experienced overseas worker knows when it's time to leave. There are many other exciting and positive situations to discover in the world of overseas employment.

Also, sometimes a situation can change suddenly—a war breaks out, or threatens to—causing you to reassess. Imminent danger is, of course, a legitimate reason to make a decision to leave a location, even if it has been satisfactory in every way up to that point.

What It's Like Living and Working Overseas

The experiences you have living and working overseas will vary greatly, depending in equal parts on your employment setting, the country in which you are living, and, of course, your own attitudes regarding new cultures. If you go overseas expecting everything to operate as it does in the United States, you most likely will be disappointed. But if the differences are what excite you, then you will need very little time to adjust to your new environment. Throughout the pages to come, in addition to learning about the different job opportunities abroad, you will hear firsthand accounts from Western "expats" (expatriates) experienced at living and working overseas.

Who's Hiring

Hiring bodies include private, U.S.-based companies with overseas interests; U.S. and foreign educational institutions; U.S. and foreign medical facilities; U.S. government agencies, departments, and programs operating abroad; U.S. armed forces departments that hire civilians; and foreign companies and other foreign government agencies that depend upon and utilize Western expertise.

Private Enterprise

U.S.-based companies including manufacturers, the aviation industry, the oil industry, engineering firms, hotels, and the like all depend on U.S. experts to staff a variety of positions vital to their overseas interests. Required qualifications will vary, of course, depending upon the area of expertise employers are seeking. Salary and benefit packages are usually quite attractive. See Chapter 3 for more information on opportunities with private enterprises.

Educational Institutions

U.S. school teachers and other educational staff (librarians, guidance counselors, principals, and other administrative staff) as well as language teachers are highly sought after in a variety of overseas educational settings.

International schools and Department of Defense Dependents Schools abound throughout the world and regularly need certified educators to staff a variety of subject areas. Private foreign and U.S.-run language centers require professional English as a Foreign Language (EFL) teachers, as do foreign universities. Opportunities for educators are covered in Chapters 4, 5, and 7.

Medical Jobs

Throughout the world, and especially in developing countries, there is a strong need for qualified medical personnel. Settings include foreign hospitals, clinics, U.S. embassies, schools, and private companies. There are jobs working with the Department of Defense Dependents Schools, the International Committee of the Red Cross or various national Red Cross agencies, and the Foreign Service. Or you can volunteer with the Peace Corps or the United Nations.

Contact the particular organization or private company with which you are interested in working. Resources are provided in the following chapters and in the appendixes.

Federal Jobs

The federal government has technical, administrative, and supervisory employment opportunities overseas. These positions are usually in the competitive federal service, and as vacancies occur, positions are filled, in most cases, by transferring career federal employees from the United States. Only when federal employees are not available for transfer overseas and qualified U.S. citizens cannot be recruited locally are these vacancies filled through the open examination process.

Individuals may also apply directly to federal agencies for excepted service positions such as attaché, office clerk-translator, translator, interpreter, Foreign Service, and Department of State positions.

Federal agencies that employ individuals overseas or utilize the services of subsidized volunteers include, but are not limited to, the following agencies:

Department of Agriculture
Department of Commerce
Department of Defense
Department of State (the Foreign Service)
Agency for International Development (AID)
Peace Corps
United Nations

U.S. Armed Forces

The Department of the Air Force, the Department of the Army, and the Department of the Navy all have various programs and positions staffed by civilian workers. Jobs range from highly technical positions to administrative and support staff.

Overseas Salaries and Other Perks

For many, the decision to go overseas is based strictly on the financial arrangements—what kind of package is being offered.

Salaries and benefits vary depending on the employer—whether you will be working for an American enterprise or a foreign one—the type of work you'll be doing, and the country in which you'll be doing it.

What follows is a list of the various forms of compensation about which you should ask any potential employer. Not all will be provided by every employer, but knowing what is possible—and what is acceptable to you—will help you through the decision-making process.

Base Salaries

Don't expect to be offered an overly glamorous salary just because you are traveling overseas. Some situations, in Europe or in Africa, for example, provide little more than a living allowance along with housing and transportation. The Persian Gulf generally offers much higher salaries, but even those base salaries might seem low at first, until you calculate all the other add-ons. Beginning EFL teachers (see Chapter 4), for example, might start at around $25,000 to $30,000 a year. Other professionals, such as pilots and engineers, can make much more—$75,000, $80,000, even $100,000.

Some employers will add an increment to the base salary, depending on the number of years of experience you have in the field or on the specific qualifications or degrees you have earned. This increases the real value of the base salary substantially. But make sure that the formula used to calculate where you fall on the scale is clear to you and that your experience has been accurately evaluated. If your contract is for longer than a year, it is usual to expect a provision for yearly raises.

Income Tax Liability

Many expatriates working overseas enjoy freedom from paying U.S. income tax. The exception to this is if you are working for the Foreign Service or other U.S. government agencies.

To qualify for this tax-free status, you would need to earn less than $70,000 per year and fulfill either the IRS's Physical Presence Test, which requires 330 full days of work during any period of 12 months in a row out of the United States; or Bona Fide Residence, which is your intention to make your home in a foreign country. Because tax laws are subject to change, double-check with the IRS before you go.

Although you might be exempt from paying U.S. income tax, you'll still have to file your returns. Most U.S. embassies have the appropriate tax forms on hand and often make tax consultants available to help expatriates fill them out.

In other countries in which you could work, you might be required to pay local income taxes. This is something you need to take into consideration when calculating the real value of your salary.

Housing

Not all positions abroad offer free accommodations, and if that is the case with a job you are considering, check to see if the employer will at least provide you with leads in the apartment hunt.

Other positions do provide housing, the kind of accommodations varying from job to job and country to country. Desert oil-rig workers might share basic housing in prefab porta-cabins. City workers could be housed in apartments or villas. On compounds typically found in the Persian Gulf, homes often mimic American suburban-style living. As a rule of thumb, the higher the status the position carries, the better the accommodations.

Furnishings

What is provided in the way of furnishings, again, varies from job to job. Some employers will supply at least the basic pieces: beds, tables, lamps, and so forth. If not, they might provide a furniture allowance.

Before you go, check to see if kitchen items, bedding, and towels are part of the package. If they are not, it usually is cheaper to buy what you need overseas rather than have everything shipped from home. How you approach this most probably will be affected by the shipping allowance you are given, if any.

Utilities

Some jobs include the cost of utilities as part of the housing benefit; in other situations you will be responsible for your own electric, gas, telephone, Internet access, and possibly, water bills.

Food

Just as with housing and other benefits, food is sometimes part of the package, especially for those working at sea or in situations where kitchen facilities are not available. Most employees, though, usually pay for their own food.

Air Tickets

If you have been hired in the United States to work for a concern overseas, then you should expect to receive air tickets for both the beginning and end of your contract. If you have found a job while already overseas, chances are your transportation home will be your own responsibility. The same holds true for vacation tickets. Most American and foreign enterprises recruiting Westerners are prepared to offer at least one vacation ticket a year, while local hires are on their own.

Vacation Leave

The amount of vacation time per year can be more generous than you'd find starting a new job at home. Although university and school teachers, for example, are traditionally the lowest-paid professionals, they make up for that with longer vacation times. Anywhere from 60 to 90 days of vacation are customary, and there are numerous day- and week-long holidays and term breaks throughout the year.

On any job, 30 days' annual leave would be the minimum to expect, or accept, unless, of course, you are a local hire.

Baggage Allowances

Your employer might provide you with a baggage allowance for the cost of shipping 50 kilograms on up, increasing with the number of dependents they have agreed to subsidize. Make sure there is some provision for getting your belongings home again when it's time to leave.

Local Transportation

Some jobs will provide their employees, usually the higher-ups, with a transportation allowance or company car. In other situations you will have to fend for yourself.

Medical Benefits

U.S. government workers and other Americans working for foreign enterprises are afforded varying degrees of medical coverage in hospitals and clinics. If this is not part of your benefits package, then you can make arrangements with your own insurance company for traveling or living-abroad coverage, or you can check with the embassy of the country to which you are heading to see what medical benefits, if any, are provided to noncitizens.

Allowances for Dependents

If you are married and want your family to relocate with you, the first thing to make sure of is that your job is offering you a "married status" position. Some companies will take on employees in only a "single status" capacity, meaning that they won't provide housing or tickets for your family or won't allow them to accompany you, even if you are willing to pay for it.

If the position is for married status, you can expect to receive beginning- and end-of-contract tickets and annual leave tickets for your spouse and, generally, up to three children.

If your family does accompany you, make sure some sort of education allowance is provided. There are a number of very good international schools around the world that operate on the American or British system, with qualified teachers from both those countries, but tuition costs are high.

End-of-Contract Gratuity

Many companies provide a standard bonus of one month's salary for every year of service. Sometimes a straight percentage of your yearly salary could be tacked on at the end of service. However, some companies offer bonuses only if you stay a minimum of two years—even if you start out with just a one-year (renewable) contract.

Other Allowances

Some concerns, especially U.S. government enterprises, offer an additional hardship allowance for certain countries and a COLA—cost of living allowance. This can add another 10, 20, or even 30 percent to your annual income.

What Does It All Add Up To?

In general, if you are hired in this country for a job overseas, you may be offered a tax-free salary with enough add-on benefits to make the job offer more than attractive. If you opt instead to go overseas first and then look for employment, you will find fewer additional benefits, such as local and international transportation and housing provided.

For many, though, the main benefit is the opportunity to travel and to live and work overseas. This can far outweigh the attractive salary package that usually accompanies professional positions abroad.

2

FINDING THAT JOB

IF YOU ARE concerned that to work overseas you'd need to pack up and travel to a foreign destination and find a job once you get there, you can put your mind at rest. Most of the professional overseas positions traditionally held by U.S. workers are usually filled via the application and interviewing processes conducted on home soil.

However, if you prefer the freedom of traveling and finding work from stop to stop, this route is still possible in some countries and for some types of jobs, such as part-time work, student jobs, or in some situations, teaching positions. How you go about instigating an overseas working experience for yourself will depend on how much security—and how much freedom—you need.

Throughout this book there is information on how to find work with various agencies and programs. In this chapter you will find general suggestions on how to broaden your job search beyond the opportunities described here.

Job-Hunting Avenues

The specific skills you possess and how much in demand they are will, in part, determine how successful your job hunt is. Engineers, scientists, computer experts, teachers, nurses and other medical personnel, skilled technicians, pilots, architects, and a score of other professionals have consistently found suitable work overseas.

Each profession has its own websites, networking circles, professional journals, recruiting fairs, continuing education seminars, and conferences; it is often through these avenues that job seekers learn about potential openings.

In addition, there are employment agencies, government departments, and private businesses that hire a variety of people skilled in different areas. What follows is a general look at the various arenas that can be approached in your overseas job search.

Electronic Databases

If you have access to the Internet, you can take advantage of all kinds of Web-based resources, from bulletin boards to listings posted on the websites of employment agencies, companies, government agencies, and more.

Searches using key words such as "jobs," "overseas," and "teaching" will likely generate hundreds of hits. It is simpler, of course, to visit any of the sites listed in this book (such as overseasjobs .com/index.htm) and to look at other books written specifically about searching for jobs using the Internet, such as *The Guide to Internet Job Searching* by Margaret Riley Dikel and Frances E. Roehm. A few clicks of your mouse will bring you to a list of job categories and the overseas openings in each of them, along with information on how to apply.

Professional Journals and Newsletters

Subscribing to professional and trade journals in your field will help to keep you abreast of opportunities. Often these publications are part of membership with particular professional associations. Many professional associations often maintain job banks as well and can refer you to appropriate openings.

If you are in college or graduate school, ask your department head for the names and addresses of related professional associations. Yearly student memberships are generally inexpensive and offer you a wealth of information. In addition, the professional associations related to opportunities covered in this book are provided for you in Appendix A.

Job Fairs and Professional Conferences

Many professions benefit from annual and semi-annual conferences sponsored by associated professional organizations. In addition to speakers and seminars designed to enhance your skills or knowledge base, many conferences also set aside room for recruiters to examine résumés and interview potential job candidates. Check with related professional associations for conference announcements. Remember to bring copies of your résumé to distribute. A passport-sized photo of yourself clipped to each résumé will help interviewers remember you when they return to their headquarters and start the job selection process.

Classified Ads

Relying on classified ads in your local newspaper isn't generally enough of an approach to guarantee success in your job search—but having said that, many people do still find jobs that way. In addition to your local newspaper or major ones such as the *Wall Street Journal*, the *New York Times*, or the *Washington Post* (available at libraries or out-of-town newspaper dealers), there is a slew of dailies and weeklies that focus solely on the different job markets. Most newsstands in large bookstore chains stock a good selection of these.

Employment Agencies

There are basically two types of employment agencies: those that are government run and offer job listings and placement services for free; and those that are private and charge either the applicant or the recruiter, or both, for matching candidates to jobs.

State Employment Offices

As a matter of course, many private companies and government bodies list their job openings with the state employment office where they are headquartered. In addition, potential overseas employers involved in various projects are encouraged by the U.S. Department of Labor to post their openings with the nationwide Interstate Job Bank. The local office of your state employment agency will have access to any of these jobs advertised.

Federal Personnel Offices

Contact the U.S. Office of Personnel Management (OPM) at opm.gov to find information about current employment and career opportunities; special programs for students, veterans, and people with disabilities; the Presidential Management Intern Program; and salaries and benefits. OPM also provides current employment information through USAJOBS, the federal government's official job site, at usajobs.opm.gov.

Private Employment Agencies

Private employment agencies are listed in most phone books. They also often announce job openings in a variety of newspapers and periodicals, as well as on electronic bulletin boards and through electronic database services. To find out the actual employer, you need to contact the agency and submit your application for work to that employer through the agency.

With private employment agencies there is always some type of fee involved. Some agencies will charge you a small, up-front fee to distribute your résumé to employers who have listed with them, and then, once you have been offered and have accepted an overseas job, they will charge you a larger fee. Others might charge you a small, up-front processing fee, but the larger placement fee is picked up by the employer.

Many employment agencies are long established and engage in only legitimate business practices. However, there are always reports of unscrupulous practices and promises of employment that never materialize; the scam often goes undiscovered until the victims have quit their jobs and sold their homes. Check with the Better Business Bureau before engaging in any transaction with an employment agency.

Direct Contact

There are many private companies and businesses headquartered in the United States that have worldwide sites of operation. The Internet and the reference desk at the library are good resources for locating these companies. Once armed with addresses and phone numbers, you can begin your direct-contact job hunt. Call the personnel office of each company—many will have 24-hour telephone job lines that list openings and give application instructions.

Embassies

If there is a particular country in which you would prefer to work, try contacting the Washington-based embassy of that country and ask for the commercial, educational, cultural, or business section. Foreign enterprises, both private and government, in search of U.S. expertise will often list their job openings with their embassies.

Adding to Your Skills Bank

Improving your chances for finding a suitable job overseas sometimes involves upgrading your skills or adding new ones. Although many job situations overseas do not require knowledge of a foreign language, being fluent or having a working knowledge of another language will greatly enhance your résumé—and your chances of landing a job in a competitive market.

Here's another point to keep in mind: finding your first overseas job might seem like a daunting task, but once you have "broken in," so to speak, the next job and the one after that will be much easier to locate and to nail down. Being able to add overseas experience to your résumé always moves you higher up the competitive ladder for future jobs.

3

Private U.S. Companies Overseas

There are thousands of U.S.-based companies that either have their own business concerns established in other countries or that contract their services to other companies or government agencies and departments with overseas connections. Locations for jobs with U.S.-based firms with overseas activities are literally worldwide and include North and South America, Asia and the Pacific, Eastern and Western Europe, Africa, and the Middle East. General methods for locating these companies were covered in Chapter 2.

Subcontracting

One way to identify companies with overseas operations is to contact organizations that either award contracts or offer assistance on locating projects that need contractors. Armed with a list of companies that have been awarded contracts, the individual in search of employment can get a jump start on the competition.

Small Business Administration

The U.S. Small Business Administration (SBA) maintains an "answer desk" to provide general information on how it can help potential exporters and service providers take advantage of overseas opportunities, including providing information on international trade or procurement and government contracting assistance. The SBA's home page (sba.gov) contains much helpful information, and the answer desk has its own page (sba.gov/answerdesk.html).

Those interested in subcontracting opportunities can enter their names in the Procurement Automated Source System (PASS), a computerized directory listing detailed profiles of more than 200,000 small business firms with interests in government contracts. Prime contractors also can use this directory to locate small business sources.

U.S. Army Corps of Engineers (USACE)

The U.S. Army Corps of Engineers regularly awards contracts to different firms involved in overseas projects. You may obtain a list of the contract awards from them, then contact the firms directly. The USACE also maintains an excellent website at usace.army.mil where information about contracts and business partnerships can be found. You might also want to contact the Commerce Business Daily at http://cbdnet.gpo.gov for information about upcoming, not-yet-awarded contracts.

Types of Jobs

The different kinds of jobs available with private U.S.-based companies run the gamut from engineers and computer specialists to administrators, managers, and sales personnel. But most jobs are skilled, professional positions and require a high level of expertise. Following are some sample job listings:

Position: Manufacturing Director, Diesel Generators

Location: Saudi Arabia

Company: Manufacturer of power generation equipment and diesel-engine-driven products within the Kingdom of Saudi Arabia.

Description: Seeking a director of manufacturing to be responsible for entire engineering and manufacturing operation. Candidates should be mechanical engineers, with a minimum of five years' managerial experience and a proven track record in designing, building, and testing of medium- and high-voltage power units, using large-bore slow/medium speed diesel engines, coupled with associated control and distribution equipment. A knowledge of ISO requirements as well as MRP concepts and application, together with the ability to interpret technical specifications and drawings and figure realistic cost estimates, are required. Management skills, team-building ability, and the leadership qualities to galvanize people at all levels to give their best are essential.

Benefits: An attractive tax-free salary will be offered, along with family status, free furnished accommodations, transport, medical insurance, and paid airfares.

———

Position: Control Systems Maintenance Specialist

Location: Indonesia

Base salary: $70,000 to $90,000

Company: Large gas producing company is seeking a B.S.-qualified engineer with 15–25 years' experience in maintenance of oil/gas industry process controls, including PLCs, DCS, etc. We have a giant gas producing field in Kalimantan, Indonesia, and this position is for the expat who will be in charge of setting up an instrument maintenance department (preventive/predictive) for all control systems in the producing fields. Candidates should know turbine and compressor controls, including such systems as Dresser-Rand, Solar, Woodward, Bently Nevada vibration monitors, Allen-Bradley PLCs, etc.

Benefits: A long-term family status position will be offered, based in Jakarta with a 28/28 rotation to the producing fields. In addition to the base salary, a large markup will be paid, which often will allow the individual to bank his or her base salary.

Positions: Electrical Engineer, Manager—4 positions

Location: Africa

Description: People are needed to fill the following four positions: A general manager with a specialty in particleboard production. An electrical engineer for a particleboard company who is conversant with SPS control machines and has a knowledge of wood processing sector. A manager of export processing/free trade zone. A general manager for a company involved in electrical contracting specializing in the supply and installation of low- and high-voltage switchgear, process control, and instrumentation; industrial, commercial, and domestic installations; and overhead reticulations.

Benefits: A competitive salary of $85,000 to $100,000 will be offered along with a superior benefit plan to include relocation and the opportunity to grow professionally in a fast-developing business environment.

Salary and Benefits

As examined in Chapter 1 and subsequent chapters, salaries and benefit packages vary from job to job and employer to employer but are usually quite comfortable. Most employees will receive transportation or reimbursement, free housing or housing allowances, and a tax-free status.

According to Steve Negley, a self-employed computer programmer and analyst who lived and worked overseas for 13 years, "Salaries were generally good—comparable to what I would be looking for in a U.S. job—but that meant you were fairly wealthy in all the places I went at that time. I got fairly standard benefits, again comparable to a U.S. job, which consisted mainly of health insurance and some retirement benefits, which I never stayed long enough to care about. The main benefit was just being overseas."

Lisa Eagleson-Roever had the opportunity to work overseas for Dowty Rotol (now Dowty Aerospace Propellers) in Gloucester, England, while she was in graduate school. Lisa offers some very specific memories of her work in England: "The system was to pay in cash—that's right, in cash. They didn't have direct deposit, and to pay by check would probably have caused a lot of inconvenience to their workers, because most everything was done in cash there. Credit cards weren't used very often, and neither were checks, except maybe to pay utility bills and the TV tax bills. (Yes, you were taxed for owning a TV!)

"I had to sign up for the National Health system, and 12 percent of my pay was deducted toward that. My health card showed up five days before I left the country."

What the Work Is Like

According to Steve, "The typical day on the job overseas was not a lot different from the typical day on the job in the United States. The principal difference was that you were in a small minority, surrounded by people of another country, or countries. Usually they spoke better English than I spoke their language, and business was conducted in English. There were miscommunications, and it was necessary to be both careful and patient in issuing instructions, but probably no more so than is required of a good supervisor or manager anywhere.

"Office facilities, supplies, and equipment tended to be less plush and less plentiful. In some places I had to buy my own pens, pencils, and erasers and also pads of paper to avoid using loose sheets of newsprint.

"Local nationals competed fiercely for jobs with U.S. companies, not only because of better pay, but also because they were treated much better. Local companies often treated employees harshly, and their supervisors required daily groveling just to keep their jobs. The supervisors, in turn, had to grovel to their bosses."

Recreation

What do expats do to occupy themselves? For many expats, leisure time (and there is plenty of it) can be spent lying on the beach, diving the coral reefs, barbecuing at the beach, attending dinner theater, or dancing until dawn.

At many locations the list of activities reads like a travelogue. As with most things in life, being willing to try new things (at least once) will make all the difference. This is how you expand your circle and meet other expats from different companies and other countries. If you put yourself out just a little and make the effort to participate, you'll find a social life busier than you ever imagined. Turn up your nose at an invitation to go square dancing or to help out with an amateur theater production, and you will end up home alone.

Steve emphasizes to remember that "off the job there always seems to be thousands of interesting things to do, and each outing seems like an adventure. Going to the beach in Vietnam or Venezuela is not like going to the beach in Venice, California. A trip to Colonia Tovar outside Caracas or to Heidelberg from Frankfurt is not at all like driving to Carmel or Pismo Beach from Los Angeles."

Culture

Despite the fact that American brands such as McDonald's, Starbucks, and KFC are ubiquitous the world over, cultural differences remain. It is possible that you will relish some of these differences and be disturbed by others.

Steve says, "Particularly in Latin America, people seem to be happier, more open, more relaxed, and friendlier than people here. It may have been superficial, but it was nevertheless pleasant and made it easier to meet and talk to people, and a party could be organized almost any time, any place. Perhaps it was just that I was less inhibited myself that made the difference. In any case, I plan to return overseas to live. My wife is a Mexican citizen, and we have been planning for some time to move to Mexico. Lately, however, all the drug-related violence has caused us to consider the possibility of Belize or Costa Rica as a permanent home, but we will probably move to Mexico first and investigate the others from there. I plan to do some computer consulting and training for U.S. firms to supplement our income."

Steve was "endlessly fascinated" by talking to people of all types and backgrounds. "Many local professionals seem to enjoy talking with foreigners, and so you get invited to a lot of social functions that you might not at home. There is also usually an expatriate community, with either its own clubs (e.g., American Theatre Club in Caracas, German Clubs almost everywhere), or access to local social and sporting clubs (e.g., Cercle Sportif in Saigon) where expatriates and upper-class local nationals gather."

Similarly, Lisa found many aspects of Gloucester charming and the people to be generous and warm, but other aspects of that community's culture both surprised and disturbed her. One involved the subtle differences between women's and men's roles. Lisa remembers, "The ladies went to lunch five minutes before the men —it was customary. Men and women never ate at the same tables together—again, this was customary. I never really understood why, but that was just the way things were. No one seemed slighted over it, but I did meet a woman from Germany who also found it a little odd.

"The work week in Britain was 37.5 hours, so the day ended a littler earlier than it does in the United States. We clocked in and out, and the end of the day was proclaimed with a very British (at least to my ears) buzzer. Again, the women were allowed to leave five minutes earlier than the men. I assume it was so that they would have less traffic to deal with (or could get on the earliest bus that came by in the evening) so that they could get home to make tea (supper) for their families. I took the bus home."

Another aspect of the culture that made her uncomfortable was that of class in British society. "I was very discouraged that the class system, although 'officially' defunct, was actually quite strong. There was an undercurrent of it everywhere. Time after time I heard people say that they could never attain some dream or another because it wasn't possible to leave 'their level.' One man very earnestly assured me that he could never start his own business and make his fortune unless he left Britain and went to America, because only in America could a man start his own business and make a million dollars. He said that people like him weren't allowed to start businesses; they'd be shut down from those above. It seemed to me (rightly or wrongly) that ambition was entirely lacking in the average person; everything would always be the way it had been because that was the way things were supposed to be. I was very glad to be an American and to have been raised differently when I noticed this trend in the people I met."

Advice

Steve concludes, "Only go overseas if you like change and can adapt to different ways of doing things. If you insist on living exactly the same as you would in the United States, you will be disappointed and unhappy in most places. The food is different, housing is different, customs are different, language is usually different, and you are a guest in a foreign country. It is up to you to adjust to the country and its customs. It is no one's obligation to adjust to our whims and preferences based on a U.S. lifestyle.

"It is especially important to be tolerant of differences in work ethics and to avoid getting angry (don't be the ugly American!) when people fail to respond in a Type A manner, or as you would expect them to in Los Angeles or New York. While service can be very good in some places and in some situations, people in many countries are not as driven and compulsive about commitments— especially time commitments—as we are in the United States. If you can't live without the customary American conveniences, you'd better stay home, or at least find the local Hilton. If you don't leave the hotel, you may feel at home, which, of course, defeats the whole point of being overseas.

"Savor the experience, the culture, the differences; try to understand the people, their customs, their dreams and aspirations. You will be back in the old familiar rat race all too soon anyway.

"As far as getting a job overseas, check the want ads regularly in the Los Angeles, New York, and Miami papers, especially the overseas editions. Check the library for foreign newspapers and magazines: England, Ireland, Australia, Hong Kong, South Africa, any others whose language you can read. Check the Internet; there are dozens of sites with job information. Don't forget the newsgroups related to your job interests.

"And, of course, if you file a declaration with the IRS that you will be overseas for 18 months or more, you avoid U.S. income tax withholding.

"The only downsides are that once in a great while you might get a craving for a real Big Mac; medical facilities may be marginal, especially if you have small kids; it can be tiring always to speak and hear another language, especially if you aren't around native English speakers for some part of the day or week; and sometimes you just really want to watch your favorite TV show in English."

Lisa considers her experience working abroad to have been very positive. She advises, "If you can get a job overseas, take it. The experience is valuable beyond measure.

"Learn as much of the language as possible before you go. If you can't learn much, then learn those phrases that will get you around a city and to the various offices you'll need to get to in order to properly register to work. Do register if you need to; the last thing you want to have as your primary memory of a country is being thrown out of it for being an undocumented, or improperly documented, alien.

"Also remember that you are now the foreigner. Learn as many of the customs as you can before you go—especially gestures. What means 'okay' in the United States may be a deadly insult somewhere else.

"Don't let someone pull you into an argument about politics unless you are truly well grounded on United States policy regarding that country. It's best to claim to be unfamiliar with the topic at hand and be as interested as possible in the other person's opinion—and keep your own mouth primly closed.

"Talk to as many different kinds of people as possible and you will learn things you never imagined there were to learn. Pay attention to how the society is structured, who defers to whom and why. This will save you no end of social embarrassment. But do not be afraid to ask discreet questions; people will generally tell you what's what and be relieved that you want to know because you will save them some possible measure of embarrassment also."

4

TEACHING ENGLISH AS A FOREIGN LANGUAGE

ONE OF THE most frequently sought-after overseas jobs is teaching English as a foreign language. At one time it was believed that the only qualification necessary to teach English to non-native speakers was to be a native speaker yourself. But these days that school of thought has almost vanished. Before the Teachers of English to Speakers of Other Languages (TESOL) profession had firmly established itself as an important and valid discipline, an individual could venture overseas and find teaching work along the way to cover travel costs and living expenses. Although these situations of tutoring and part-time teaching do still exist in a few locations, they are quickly shrinking and being replaced with quality programs touting qualified and experienced ESL/EFL teachers.

TESOL is a professional organization of trained and experienced teachers who have made teaching ESL/EFL a long-term career. They have studied in accredited programs, working toward certification, bachelor's, and master's degrees. They are familiar with up-to-date teaching methodology and classroom materials, and they have acquired an awareness of other cultures and are sensitive to their differences.

What Is EFL?

EFL stands for English as a foreign language; TEFL for teaching English as a foreign language. Recipients of this course of instruction may live in a country where their own language is the primary tongue; English may be used for academic study or in preparation for travel to an English-speaking country or for business purposes.

What Makes a Good EFL Teacher?

Teaching English as a second or foreign language is not the same as teaching it as a first language. There is a foundation of knowledge and methodology for this field of study that includes linguistics, second-language acquisition, education practices, sociology, anthropology, psychology, testing and measurement, and other related subjects.

In addition to a strong foundation in the above-mentioned areas, EFL teachers must have a special talent; they carry a weighty responsibility. How they present their subject will affect their students' attitudes toward language learning—the English language in particular—and also toward the teachers' country and its culture.

EFL teachers need to possess the same qualities that any teachers do: intelligence, patience, and creativity. They also have to have an understanding of the nature of language in general and how people learn languages. They must have cross-cultural knowledge and experience and be sensitive to individual differences among students. In certain settings, they must also have knowledge of other areas related to international student affairs, such as immigration and visa policies.

These additional qualities are helpful to a successful career as a teacher of English as a second or foreign language:

- Experience traveling or living in international settings
- Enthusiasm for the subject matter
- Independence
- A sincere appreciation of people from different cultures
- Ability to work as part of a team
- Tolerance
- Flexibility
- Maturity
- Communication skills

A successful EFL teacher also maintains an interest in continuing professional development and helps to encourage the same interest in those he or she supervises, including other teachers and staff members.

But does a successful EFL teacher need to be a native speaker of English? Although a small contingent might argue for that requirement, most believe that it is an elitist attitude that should have no place in the field of TESOL. Why should every non-English-speaking country in the world have to depend on English-speaking ones for its EFL instruction? A teacher from France, for example, with a solid command of the English language and professional qualifications from a recognized TESOL program, is ultimately better equipped to help students in his or her own country understand the process of learning English. Such a teacher would be more aware of the nuances, the specific French-to-English problems students would have than would a native English speaker.

But what if the teacher is tempted to speak French in the classroom to help a student over a rough spot? If the method of instruction is direct English to English, the resolution of this question can be highly charged. Most instructors agree that English should be the language of instruction in an EFL classroom, but many don't see the harm—in fact, can see the benefit—of an occasional quick translation to clear up points of confusion for the students. Why waste precious classroom time when a quick aside allows everyone to move on?

What an EFL Teacher Does

Many people not yet in the profession believe that since they can speak English they should, therefore, be able to teach it. As mentioned earlier, in some locations that's true, and often travelers wanting to earn extra money to help pay for their trip find work tutoring or providing practice in conversation skills. But as the number of professionally trained teachers increases, opportunities for unqualified teachers decrease.

Professional EFL teachers go through a variety of training programs, studying methodology, second-language acquisition, curriculum design, research methods, and basic language skills. They might also add particular specializations to their program such as computer-assisted language learning (CALL) or the use of the Internet or videos in the classroom.

EFL teachers instruct students in basic English language skills: reading, writing, listening, and conversation. Like any teachers, they are responsible for designing lesson plans and for administering and grading tests. They might also help develop the teaching program that will best meet their particular students' needs, select textbooks, and even write materials to be used in the classroom.

The actual duties an EFL teacher will be assigned depends, in part, on the institution in which he or she works, but there are some responsibilities that are common to all settings. An EFL teacher will be responsible for a certain number of classes and will be expected to teach those classes for a certain number of hours per week. During class time, the EFL teacher will be expected to keep track of daily attendance, follow a syllabus, and create and present exercises and activities that facilitate learning. EFL teachers will also be responsible for the atmosphere in the classroom; enthusiasm and command of the subject matter should help motivate and inspire confidence in the students. EFL teachers also will be expected to manage any discipline problems that occur.

Outside of classroom hours, EFL teachers will be expected to maintain a certain number of office hours to be available to students who have questions and/or problems. Office hours might be used to provide students with extra tutoring as needed. The rest of the working hours will be spent designing lesson plans, developing supplemental or primary materials for use in the classroom, writing and grading quizzes and exams, correcting homework assignments, and meeting with coordinators and other teachers in the program. EFL teachers might also be expected to devote an hour or so a week to supervising language laboratory or library/learning resource center activities.

Workload

Generally teachers are contracted to work the academic year, from August or September through May or June. Depending upon the institution, your salary might be for nine months or the full year. This leaves anywhere from 60 to 90 days free for paid or unpaid vacation time. The exception to that are teachers employed by private language centers or businesses that do not follow an academic year. Then vacation time might be 30 or 45 days, usually paid.

Primary and secondary school teachers generally work the same schedule as teachers in the United States. University teachers might have a lighter teaching schedule than school teachers, but they still juggle 10 to 25 hours a week of classroom teaching with curriculum design, student conferences, materials writing, committee meetings, and the like.

Teachers in private language schools often have the heaviest workload, teaching anywhere from 25 to 40 hours a week. Sometimes they are responsible for a split shift, teaching classes from 8:00 A.M. to noon and then from 4:00 to 8:00 P.M. This can make the day even longer.

Coordinators and supervisors generally teach fewer hours but fill their time with administrative duties including scheduling, writing course materials and exams, and handling any of the problems that might arise.

Employment Outlook

It's estimated that more than one billion people around the world speak or are learning how to speak English. They choose to learn English for a number of reasons: to attend colleges and universities in English-speaking countries, to ensure better business communications, to enhance employability, to facilitate government relations, to create a more rewarding travel experience, or for many, to be able to communicate day-to-day in the English-speaking country in which they live.

It can be assumed that the need for English language instruction is increasing worldwide. As the public school systems, government agencies, and private enterprises continue to work toward filling the demand, opportunities for EFL teachers will continue to grow.

Job Settings for EFL Teachers

As the need for English language instruction increases, so does the variety of locations in which EFL teachers work. TESOLers are finding their skills more and more in demand and the better their qualifications, the better their employment outlook.

EFL teachers can find employment almost anywhere, although the largest concentration of jobs outside the United States appear to be in the Far East, in countries such as Japan, Hong Kong, China, and South Korea; in Central and Eastern Europe, in Turkey and Poland; in North Africa, in Egypt and Morocco; in Middle Eastern countries such as Saudi Arabia; and in the many countries of Central and South America.

The most common settings for EFL teachers are private or government-run (both U.S. and foreign) language centers and foreign universities and U.S. universities with overseas programs.

EFL teachers also work overseas in international schools (see Chapter 5), for overseas companies or private U.S. companies with overseas concerns, for the Peace Corps (see Chapter 7), or for U.S. government centers for English language instruction based around the world.

U.S. Government–Sponsored Centers and Programs

Stated simply, part of the foreign policy of the U.S. government is to aid developing countries and encourage and support the use of the American educational system overseas. In addition, the U.S. government needs to provide education for dependents of its overseas personnel. With those goals in mind, the U.S. government supports or directly funds a number of programs that regularly hire TESOL professionals.

U.S. Department of Defense

Elementary and secondary schools have been operating on U.S. military bases overseas since 1946. Children of military and civilian personnel attend these schools, and though most positions open are for subject teachers, as opposed to EFL teachers, occasionally there is a need for EFL instruction. Complete details for Department of Defense Dependents Schools are provided in Chapter 5.

U.S. Department of State

The Office of Overseas Schools of the U.S. Department of State provides assistance to selected independent overseas schools. There are two basic purposes for this assistance: to ensure that adequate educational opportunities exist for the dependents of U.S. personnel overseas, and to encourage schools that demonstrate American educational philosophies and practices within the countries in which they are located.

Although the relationship between American embassies and various American schools overseas may be close, the schools are all private institutions and are thus responsible for their own staff recruitment. Salary levels and benefits vary from school to school and region to region. Students are generally children of diplomats and others involved in the international community.

A partial list of these schools is available in Appendix C. For a complete list and resource guide, contact the Office of Overseas Schools at:

Office of Overseas Schools
A/OS Room 245 SA-29
Department of State
Washington, D.C. 20522-2902
state.gov/m/a/os

Teachers wishing to inquire about or apply for a position should write directly to a school's administrator.

Office of English Language Programs

There is a great need and demand for improving the training of English teachers from governments worldwide. By providing English-language teacher training programs worldwide, ultimately more peoples of the world will speak English proficiently. The thinking is that not only will mutual understanding and trust be increased, but also the U.S. government is paving the way for U.S. universities, businesses, and other organizations to flourish and further advance American interests.

The Office of English Language Programs is a State Department program administered by the Bureau of Educational and Cultural Affairs (which can be found on the Web at exchanges.state.gov) to further these goals. The office creates and implements high-quality, targeted English language and culture programs in specific regions and countries of the world. Officers plan, conduct, and support programs sponsored by American embassies and consulates.

The office oversees two exchange programs for English language teachers. Details about the programs can be found on its website. The two programs are: the English Language Fellow Program, currently administered by the School for International Training, for recent American TESL/TEFL graduates and for experienced teacher trainers ("senior" fellows); and the English Language Specialist program, which annually sends about 75 academics overseas for short-term programs.

Regional English Language Officers (RELOs)

The office has a staff of regional English language officers (RELOs), program specialists, and support staff based in Washington and overseas. All RELOs hold advanced academic degrees in the teaching of English as a foreign language (TEFL), applied linguistics, or a related field. They have, as well, many years of experience as EFL teachers, teacher trainers, university educators, and administrators.

In the field, RELO is the U.S. government's front-line diplomatic and professional link between the English teaching profession in the United States and counterpart English teaching professionals in other countries. RELOs consult with host-country ministry, university, and teacher-training officials, as well as lecture and present workshops on EFL methodology and practices. They stimulate and reinforce academic exchange programs between the United States and other countries to help interpret American life and institutions to the world. They also provide oversight for the English teaching programs run directly by American embassies in some parts of the world and engage in consultative services for binational centers and English teaching programs affiliated with American embassies throughout the world.

Please note that RELOs cannot hire or recruit teachers directly. If you are interested in a teaching job in a specific country, you need to either contact an institution in that country directly or contact an embassy or consulate of that country for information.

The Office of English Language Programs website is full of helpful information, including a list of contacts for RELOs all over the world and a list of frequently asked questions (FAQ).

Office of English Language Programs
U.S. Department of State (Annex #44)
301 Fourth Street SW, Room 304
Washington, D.C. 20547
http://exchanges.state.gov/education/engteaching

Fulbright Program

The purpose of the Fulbright Program is to "increase mutual understanding between the people of the United States and the people of other countries." Grants are awarded (about 5,000 each year) to American scholars, students, and teachers to study, teach, and conduct research abroad. Foreign nationals are also funded to engage in similar activities in the United States.

The United States Information Agency (USIA) administers the Fulbright Program in cooperation with other federal agencies and a few private organizations.

The Fulbright Program includes Pre-Doctoral Fellowships, the Scholar-in-Residence Program, the Hubert Humphrey Fellowship Program, the University Affiliations Program, the American Scholar Program, and the Fulbright Teacher Exchange Program. The last three programs are of most interest to ESL/EFL teachers.

The American Scholar Program

This program funds over 1,000 scholars and professionals a year in more than 100 different countries. These scholars and other professionals conduct research or lecture in a wide variety of settings and academic and professional fields.

The Fulbright Teacher Exchange Program

This program creates opportunities for college faculty and elementary- and secondary-level teachers and administrators to work in selected institutions outside the United States for a semester or full academic year. Teachers must already be employed and are usually paid the same salary their current position offers. Some expenses such as airfare and housing are included.

Candidates must be U.S. citizens, have at least a bachelor's degree, and have three years of full-time teaching experience. Applications must be postmarked by October 15 for the following summer or academic year's program. Request an application packet and information on all Fulbright programs from:

The Fulbright Teacher Exchange Program
301 Fourth Street SW
Washington, D.C. 20547
fulbrightexchanges.org

USAID

The United States Agency for International Development (USAID) funds scores of programs worldwide, including education and human resources development. USAID's education and human resources development officers analyze, advise, and assist with the development of host country educational systems. Goals are to improve existing programs and to promote organizational competencies and skills acquisition. Duties include program and project design, program monitoring, and evaluation and development.

Candidates must have a graduate degree, preferably in education or related fields such as sociology, psychology, or communications. Overseas experience in a developing country is desirable. At least two years' experience is required in one or more of the following areas: educational research/evaluation, planning, policy development, administration, the economics of education, curriculum and material development, development and application of educational technology, vocational/technical education, classroom teaching, and training or supervision of teachers.

Successful candidates are appointed as interns at the Foreign Service level of 7, 6, 5, or 4. Interns must participate in a two-year training program both in Washington and overseas. Evaluations are yearly thereafter. By law, USAID must offer tenure or terminate career-candidate employees within five years of employment.

Postings are worldwide; USAID currently operates programs in approximately 70 developing countries in Africa, Asia, Latin America and the Caribbean, and the Middle East.

Further information can be obtained from USAID at:

Information Center
U.S. Agency for International Development
Ronald Reagan Building
Washington, D.C. 20523-1000
usaid.gov

Peace Corps

The Peace Corps offers interesting opportunities for people of all ages, though most new recruits are recent college graduates. EFL volunteers are expected to be qualified in the field. They work in a variety of settings, from rural or traveling classrooms to urban schools or ministries. Their duties range from straight language instruction to training future teachers to curriculum design and consulting.

Full details on volunteering with the Peace Corps in a variety of professions and capacities are provided in Chapter 7.

YMCA

The YMCA Overseas Service Corps hires young men and women with TESL/TEFL training and/or experience for positions overseas. Contact the director at:

Overseas Personnel Programs
National Board of YMCAs
291 Broadway
New York, New York 10107
ymca.net

U.S. Universities' Overseas Programs

Many United States universities and colleges set up and administer English language programs with "sister" universities overseas.
Funding for these programs come from a variety of sources such as
USAID grants or Fulbright monies or from the overseas universities themselves. EFL teachers are usually recruited in the United
States through advertisements in the *Chronicle of Higher Education*
and other publications and at the annual TESOL conference. One
example is SUNY–Buffalo, which maintains an EFL program in
Jakarta. Salaries are generally competitive and housing and airfare
are included.

Foreign Universities, Colleges, and Technical Schools

Foreign universities, colleges, and technical schools are large employers of EFL teachers. For many overseas institutions, the main
language of instruction is English, and language training is necessary to support the academic and/or technical programs. Overseas
institutions may operate entire language centers to cater to the
needs of the student population or incorporate an EFL component
into the various departments. This is common with many Middle
Eastern universities, for example, requiring intensive language training for first-year students.

Other universities might have strong English departments staffed with qualified native speakers. Salaries vary from country to country but are generally competitive and include housing and other benefits.

Universities follow the normal routes for recruitment, including advertising openings in periodicals or through agencies and conferences. More information on finding an EFL job is provided later in this chapter.

Foreign Government Agencies

Some overseas ministries of defense provide English language instruction to their military personnel. Other government departments such as education, information, or health, for example, also hire EFL teachers. Contact the appropriate embassies for addresses.

Private Language Schools

Private language centers flourish throughout the world. Although many hire teachers locally, others make far-reaching recruitment efforts. Teaching loads can run from 20 to 40 hours per week. Housing and airfare may or may not be provided.

Private Companies

Both U.S. private companies with overseas operations and foreign private companies often have an ongoing need to provide employees with English language instruction. Time is usually allocated during the employee's workday (common in Japan) to attend classes. In some situations the employee might be taken off a normal work schedule and enrolled in a training program from one to six months, or even longer (common in the Persian Gulf). Some private companies, such as ARAMCO in Saudi Arabia, also provide schooling for their employees' dependents.

Private companies also advertise their needs in the *Chronicle of Higher Education* or attend recruitment fairs. Salaries and benefits are generally competitive, with housing and transportation provided.

Teaching Conditions

Teaching environments and work conditions can vary widely. EFL teachers sometimes find themselves working in a modern classroom outfitted with state-of-the-art equipment and teaching aids—PowerPoint, DVDs, and large-screen projection systems—or in a more primitive setting with tin-roofed buildings and outdated materials, if any at all. There could be chalkboards, but no chalk; computers, but only intermittent electricity. There are numerous possibilities, and they should all be taken into account when deciding the conditions under which you would be most comfortable working. Some people get to experience both ends of the range. One of them is James McMullan. James started teaching EFL in 1978, after he graduated from the University of London with a bachelor's degree in English. He later went back to school to earn his master's degree in linguistics and language teaching and has lived and worked in England, Germany, Nigeria, Egypt, Qatar, Oman, Yemen, and California. Recently he worked in Qatar, in the Persian Gulf, for a private U.S.-based company.

James says, "In Nigeria I taught at a high school–level teacher-training college. The classroom building had a corrugated iron roof on concrete blocks, with shutters rather than windows and very dusty blackboards that were difficult to write on. Electricity wasn't always available; in the summer the transformer was down for three weeks. No air-conditioning, no fans.

"In Germany the university had beautiful, old buildings with nicely fitted classrooms. The universities in Qatar and Oman, in the Persian Gulf, were modern, purpose-built facilities with all the latest equipment. But in Qatar the male and female students were segregated from each other, and in Oman the females entered the classrooms through separate entrances and had to sit at the back of the room."

Another EFL teacher, Joanne Burch, describes her experience at the International School of Moshi in Moshi, Tanzania, in east Africa. She says, "School supplies and housing were not the best. The schoolrooms were also all cement with louvered windows, and they echoed. The 'blackboard' was a large piece of plywood that had been painted black.

"One should bring favorite textbooks, workbooks, or whatever. Books are not easy to order or to receive. Luckily, I had a couple of workbooks for each grade level I taught—middle school and high school."

Living Conditions and Lifestyle Issues

Joanne says, "Housing was provided. Mine was a two-bedroom duplex in a set of three duplexes. Two large, jalousied windows looked out into the yard from the living room. The furniture was wood, and all the walls and ceiling were cement. It echoed strangely with every word uttered.

"We were also briefed on some facts. The hospital, school, and the duplexes had pure filtered water. I would not have to boil water to drink it. Medicine and doctors were free. Two doctors and a nurse lived on campus near me. It was recommended that we not take quinine or fansadar, because the mosquitoes were becoming resistant to it. It was better to wait and see. If you got malaria, you could take quinine then.

"Telephones were also available nearby, either across campus or 'down the block.'

"The bus would take us to town on the weekend for shopping. Being without the freedom of a car was difficult for me, but I often caught rides with my neighbors—which was better than the bus. The Irish teacher and her English husband, who also had a two-year-old, often went to dinner, shopping, or on a safari and took me with them.

"Take toilet paper, a pancake turner, and any of your favorite spices. For the sake of the school, you might take sheets and a blanket. Maybe some pots and pans. Wooden spoons and so forth were available, but not too many pans and silverware.

"If you can get lightbulbs for 220 volts (not American) take them. I had one lightbulb when I first got there. So, if I was in the living room, that's where the lightbulb was. Bedtime? Unscrew the bulb and take it with you. Bath time? Don't forget the lightbulb!"

In contrast, James says, "Working in the Gulf provides a lot of opportunities for sports and camping enthusiasts. But with cable TV and the increasing availability of Internet access, indoors types are also well taken care of. There's really no way you can feel cut off from the rest of the world when your hometown newspaper is just a mouse click away, and *Wheel of Fortune* is broadcast three times a day."

James adds, "The main drawback to the work and the lifestyle is the fact that expatriate communities function very much like those gossip-filled small towns we all tried to get away from. I've found that the best way to deal with this is to maintain an interest—and a circle of friends—that are separate from my working environment.

"That way you can occasionally kick back and let off steam without fearing what your office-mates will say on Saturday morning.

"Also, learning to be flexible and tailoring what you have to offer to what your employer and the students need can be difficult. You have to look at the constraints of the particular country. For example, if you love teaching with computers or with slide projectors, be ready to adapt that approach when you move to a country that doesn't have electricity in the classrooms. Sometimes you have to throw your notions or techniques out the window and be very adaptable and sensitive. That is part of the learning you go through."

Salaries and Benefits

Salaries and benefits are also pluses, but they vary from region to region and employer to employer. ESL pay scales in the United States are usually competitive with other teachers' salaries. In general, jobs overseas in areas that offer more "hardship" to Americans, such as the Middle East, pay higher wages and provide more special allowances. In such a setting you would probably receive free housing and furniture, free travel, free medical care, and a bonus at the end of your contract. (See Chapter 1 for a detailed description of benefit packages.)

In poorer countries or in countries where the lifestyle is more compatible with what Americans are used to, salaries are generally lower.

James says, "Because my contract includes a food allowance, gas allowance, and membership in a senior staff club—which includes a fitness center—my out-of-pocket expenditures are relatively low. Most of my salary goes straight into a savings account."

Joanne's benefits were good, too. She says, "School ended at 1:30 P.M., at which time I walked across the soccer field to my clean house and a dinner that was already prepared for me. A house-keeper/cook/babysitter was part of the pay.

"I also had a gardener and night guard. The night of my arrival, I discovered my night guard. Still on Arizona time, I got up in the middle of the night for a drink of water. Half asleep, I raised my glass and looked into a grinning face outside the window. As I gasped in horror, he waved, 'I be your guard.' The guard was to prevent theft—not for defense."

Educational Preparation

Employment opportunities are wide and varied for EFL teachers, but where you'll be able to work, and to some extent, what salary you'll earn, will be determined by your qualifications. Although many people with no qualifications other than being a native English speaker report finding teaching or tutoring positions, those jobs are quickly disappearing.

As the profession grows, as it has continued to do over the last 20 years or so, and more teachers graduate from accredited train-ing programs, EFL jobs will become more competitive and will go to only qualified and experienced teachers. The more qualifications and experience you have, the better the job setting, pay scale, and benefits.

But not only does training increase your employment chances, it can help enhance your sense of confidence when facing a classroom of eager language learners. A good short-term course can provide you with the basic EFL teaching methodologies and introduce you to the latest materials.

Qualifications

It is important, when deciding on how much training you will pursue, to take into account the level of teaching you plan to do. Classroom teachers working within U.S. school systems, for example, need at least a bachelor's degree; overseas university language center instructors are expected for the most part to have earned a master's degree.

EFL teachers, as with all teachers, must be familiar with up-to-date teaching materials, classroom management methods, teaching methodology, lesson planning, and student evaluations. They also must be familiar with ESL/EFL materials, course design, teaching methods, as well as with the nature of language in general, the nature of the English language in particular (phonology, lexicon, syntax, and pragmatics), the nature of second-language acquisition, and the interaction of culture and language.

EFL professionals are also expected to demonstrate certain specialized skills that can develop through experience as well as training. This can cover various interest areas such as computer-assisted language learning or the use of the Internet in the classroom. It can expand to more administrative duties including curriculum development, course coordination, supervision of other teachers, and teacher training.

Bachelor's Degree

A bachelor's degree is considered the basic requirement for employment. If the candidate expects to go on for a master's degree, it is not necessary for the B.A. to be in TESOL. An undergraduate could major in English or foreign languages or international relations. But if the B.A. is to be the terminal degree, the program should cover courses such as the grammatical, phonological, and semantic systems of the English language; methodology and second-language assessment; the study of another language and its cultural system; and practice in teaching.

State Teachers' Certification

Certification is required in most states for teaching ESL at the elementary and secondary levels in U.S. public schools. Some U.S. government bodies such as the Department of Defense also require overseas teachers to be certified.

Contact your state board of education to learn what the certification requirements are. University teacher training programs will offer these required courses.

U.S. Certification

Many universities with education departments offer an ESL certificate that can be earned with another 18 to 21 graduate credits beyond the bachelor's degree. The U.S. certificate is considered adequate for many job settings outside the United States and would qualify you to teach adult education in private language programs or at some community colleges within the United States.

U.K. Certification

These days many American as well as British teachers are earning TEFL certificates from the University of Cambridge and Trinity College in the United Kingdom. These certificates are earned in short-term intensive programs in the United Kingdom and throughout the world. Appendix C includes a short selection of programs and their addresses. Write directly to the program of your choice for applications, deadlines, requirements, and costs.

Master's Degree

A master's degree, in addition to a theoretical background, will prepare you in classroom teaching methods, curriculum development, materials writing, and to some extent, program coordination. With a master's degree you will be qualified to teach in most settings in the United States and abroad. There are a variety of names for the different master's degrees including: M.A. in TESOL, M.Ed. in TESOL, M.A. or M.S. in applied linguistics, M.A.T. in TEWL, or an M.A. in English with an emphasis in TESOL. An employer might specify one particular degree when advertising a position but is usually willing to consider any of the variations.

Ph.D. Degree

Those wishing to advance academically and become involved in language research, writing for professional publications, and/or teaching future ESL/EFL teachers at the master's level will need to pursue a Ph.D. degree.

TESOL's *Directory of Teacher Education Programs* lists universities offering certificate, master's, and doctoral programs in TESOL in the United States, Canada, and Mexico.

Choosing a Training Program

It's a good idea to compare programs for master's degrees before making your final choice. Some are more theoretical, some are more practical, some concentrate more on international than domestic issues or vice versa; they all have a different focus.

Of the 131 master's programs surveyed, 69 percent require practical training such as student teaching, 56 percent require a comprehensive examination, 28 percent require a thesis, and 28 percent offer the thesis as an option. Average time to complete the program (attending full-time) is 4.1 semesters, and the average number of required credits is 36.4 semester hours.

Before making a serious commitment in terms of the number of years of training you will pursue, you can follow a few other options first to get a feel for the profession:

1. Volunteer your time and take advantage of any of the in-house training an organization might offer.
2. Enroll in a short-term intensive training program (several are listed in Appendix A) and work toward a certificate.
3. After finishing your bachelor's degree, spend a year or two working in the field before going on for a master's.

Whatever you choose to do, it's best to start out with a plan. If you ask a handful of longtime ESL/EFL teachers how they got started, you might hear a string of surprising answers such as "I just fell into it" or "I was traveling in Europe, and one thing just led to another." But times have changed. These days, to land the plum jobs, teachers plan their programs very carefully. They choose courses that will meet their own needs and interests, while also considering the needs and requirements of future employers.

What Employers Look for in an EFL Teacher

According to a survey TESOL conducted, questioning 153 TESOL educators and employers in 30 countries, most stressed their preference for hiring teachers with a solid background in the methods and materials used in teaching EFL.

Survey participants were asked to rate the importance of four general areas and 60 specific topics in the preparation of teachers of English as a second or foreign language. Literature, linguistics, TESOL methods, and TESOL materials were the four general areas. Methods ranked first, linguistics and education landed in the middle of the list, and literature was rated the lowest.

The top 10 in importance of the 60 specialized topics were:

1. Specific training in how to teach listening comprehension
2. Specific training in TESOL materials selection and evaluation
3. Specific training in how to teach ESL/EFL reading skills
4. Intercultural understanding
5. Practical teaching experience
6. Specific training in how to teach ESL/EFL writing skills
7. Specific training in how to teach ESL/EFL conversation skills
8. Specific training in how to teach pronunciation
9. An understanding of the language-learning process
10. A knowledge of general, introductory linguistics

International Teaching Assistants

For those not interested in completing a full course toward a degree, work is available overseas for international teaching assistants. (Often ITAs are natives of the country in which the instruction is taking place.)

A new interest group within TESOL addresses all research, teaching, and administrative issues related to the preparation of international teaching assistants for instructional duties in university classrooms. Its purpose is to promote scholarship, to disseminate research results, and to strengthen instruction. Interest in this area is blossoming, and already U.S. universities have started developing ITA training programs. Contact TESOL for more information.

Deciding Your Specialty

In addition to deciding the age and proficiency level of students with whom you prefer to work, you can opt to focus your training on a particular specialization. Although it is important for you as an ESL/EFL teacher to be a generalist, to have a solid background in every aspect of the field, it can also be helpful to your career to have more intensive training and experience in one or more particular areas.

What follows is a list of the 18 interest sections TESOL recognizes as concerns within the TESOL profession. These sections provide a focus for individual members' specializations. Membership in TESOL automatically offers affiliation with at least three of these interest sections. They are:

Applied linguistics
ESOL in adult education
ESL in bilingual education
ESOL in elementary education
ESL in secondary education
ESL in higher education
Intensive English programs
English as a foreign language
Research
Refugee concerns
Teacher education

Computer-assisted language learning
Program administration
Materials writers
Teaching English to deaf students
Video
English for specific purposes
International teaching assistants

Teaching Test Preparation

One area of the TESOL profession is providing preparation courses for students needing to take English language proficiency tests. These tests are used by administrators to help with decisions regarding admission to universities, level placement in language programs, and eligibility for educational grants and awards or certain licenses.

Some ESL/EFL instructors work only with test preparation, teaching the particular skills necessary to do well on the following exams:

• The TOEFL (Test of English as a Foreign Language) is used mainly to assess language proficiency in North American English and determine placement levels for incoming international students to U.S. universities and colleges. The test is administered monthly at official test centers around the world. It measures listening comprehension, structure and written expression, vocabulary, and reading comprehension.

• The TOEIC (Test of English for International Communication) measures listening and reading comprehension and the proficiency of non-native speakers engaged in business, commerce, and industry. The multiple-choice test is offered by request internationally.

• The TWE (Test of Written English) assesses the English writing proficiency of non-native English speakers. It is an essay test administered four times a year with the TOEFL exam. Its scores are used by undergraduate and graduate programs for admissions purposes.

The TWE measures writing skills that focus on sentence structure, syntax, the ability to present ideas in an organized fashion, and the ability to choose appropriate details to support a thesis. Here is a sample essay question: *Inventions such as eyeglasses and the sewing machine have had an important effect on our lives. Choose another important invention. Give specific reasons for your choice.*

• The TSE (Test of Spoken English) assesses spoken English proficiency. It is an oral free-response test offered 12 times a year around the world. It is used mainly to determine eligibility for graduate teaching assistantships and professional licensing. The TSE measures the candidates' skills in reading aloud, proper pronunciation and clear speech, telling a story, and answering questions.

• The SLEP (Secondary Level English Proficiency Test) assesses the English listening and reading comprehension proficiency of secondary school students who are non-native speakers of English. It is used to determine progress and readiness to enter into full-time instructional programs conducted in English. This multiple choice test is administered locally.

• The ITP (Institutional Testing Program) offers an unofficial TOEFL format exam that can be administered by individual institutions up to six times a year. Results are used for placement and admissions purposes.

Test preparation instructors work in university-based language centers, private language schools, adult education programs, and community colleges.

Learning the Language

Learning another language is not a prerequisite for most TESOL programs or for most U.S. or overseas employers. The TEFL method of instruction is direct English to English. In the United States a classroom could have students with a variety of language backgrounds. Having to learn all the different native languages would be unwieldy, to say the least.

Although learning another language is not required, to study at least one strengthens a teacher's employability. Some professionals believe that EFL teachers cannot fully understand the problems students encounter studying English unless they also have gone through the process of learning a second language themselves.

In addition, some employers overseas in countries such as Korea, Japan, or the Arabic-speaking nations give more regard to teachers who have made an effort to learn the language of the host country than to those who have not.

Although English has become the number one international language of business, it is not spoken by everyone. Knowledge of the language of the country in which you are living and working will make your stay more rewarding.

Volunteering

Volunteering is an excellent opportunity to take on new challenges, prove yourself, and enhance your effectiveness. It is also an excellent opportunity for making contacts for future employment.

For many, a stint of volunteer work in an EFL program occurs just before entering a TESOL training program or runs concurrently with the training program as a part of the curriculum. Others who are well established in the field take time out to help colleagues and cultivate new contacts.

Advantages and Disadvantages of an EFL Career

Most EFL teachers enjoy many of the same benefits of teachers of any subject—shorter working days and long summer vacations, for example. But to most EFL teachers, the main pleasure of the profession is not just the opportunity to travel, but the chance to live for long periods of time in a variety of foreign countries.

Those who opt to stay in the United States still enjoy a sort of vicarious travel by working with students from different countries.

For most teachers, the ultimate reward comes from the students themselves.

Most satisfied TESOLers will tell you that the advantages far outweigh the disadvantages, but still, these few minuses to teaching work in general should be considered:

- **Low pay.** In spite of the lucrative benefit packages and earnings and savings potential afforded to ESL/EFL teachers in some overseas locations, most teachers recognize that the salary level is far below that of other professionals such as doctors, attorneys, and engineers.
- **Stress.** How each teacher responds to stressful situations is a matter of individual temperament, but there are certain factors in the teaching profession that can lead to stress. Some of these are: handling discipline problems in the classroom, meeting a new class for the first time, overcrowded classrooms, deadlines for grading papers or handing in exam scores, and inadequate materials or facilities.

As with any profession, stress can be generated by strained relations with coworkers, work assignments outside your usual scope of duties, and occasional boredom with the subject matter.

Stress also can be brought about by change, and for EFL teachers who travel abroad, the adjustment period to a new culture and new ways of doing things can create new levels of anxiety and tension. These levels usually decrease once the settling-in period is over. Dedicated teachers learn to cope with the stress and other disadvantages; some don't even regard them as such.

Finding Your EFL Job

Seasoned TESOLers follow a series of well-proven methods that take the guesswork out of job hunting. Once a newcomer learns the ropes, finding that second or third job becomes a much simpler process.

Steps to locate employment can begin not at the end of your studies, but while you are choosing the training program you will attend. Most universities with TESOL programs have an onsite language center or offer classes to incoming international students where you can volunteer your services or be placed for practice teaching. In addition, many U.S. universities operate EFL programs with sister universities in foreign countries such as Malaysia or Indonesia. After graduation you might be able to slip into a full-time job through your own program.

Once you're enrolled in your TESOL program, try to absorb as much information as you can. Take advantage of your college or university's graduate placement office. Counselors maintain books and pamphlets on specific careers and can help guide you to the appropriate resources. Remember to discuss your plans with your professors. Most will be actively involved in the field, keeping in touch with other professionals. The contacts you make during your training program are great resources who can be invaluable for future job placement.

Joining Professional Associations

TESOL (Teachers of English to Speakers of Other Languages) is the professional association for ESL/EFL teachers. Membership, in addition to keeping you abreast of current developments in the field, will help you in your job search. The organization puts out a regular job placement bulletin for members, listing openings both in the United States and overseas.

TESOL also has for sale an introductory kit that includes an overview of the profession, required qualifications, and employment outlooks.

NAFSA (The National Association for Foreign Student Affairs), an organization serving mainly international student advisers/counselors, has a strong ESL/EFL connection. NAFSA also puts out a regular bulletin listing job openings.

Contact information for both TESOL and NAFSA are provided in Appendix A.

Locating Job Advertisements

Although standard help-wanted ads found in local newspapers might be of some help in locating employment close to home, there are specific periodicals TESOLers regularly use in their overseas employment search.

In addition to the job bulletins published by TESOL and NAFSA, there are several other good sources of EFL job listings. The *Chronicle of Higher Education*, a professional journal published weekly, advertises openings both in the United States and abroad.

Two U.K. newspapers are worth investigating as well because many overseas employers look to England to find teachers. They are the *Times Educational Supplement*, which comes out on Fridays (see Appendix B for a more complete listing) and the Tuesday edition of the *Guardian*.

Sample Job Advertisements

Below are two sample advertisements for job openings found in the above-mentioned sources:

Country: Japan

Organization: Private language institute

Position: Instructor

Duties: Teach approximately 20 periods per week in either intensive business course or nonintensive course; some administrative and residential responsibilities

Qualifications: M.A. in TESL plus two years' experience or appropriate experience in business or international relations

Location: Nice small city one hour from Tokyo, near mountains and sea

Salary: 329,000 yen per month to start, with a raise each year

Benefits: Travel paid in arrears, seven weeks' paid vacation, numerous others

Starts: Summer

Country: Spain

Organization: International Language School in Madrid

Position: ESL Instructor

Duties: Plan, teach, and evaluate assigned classes according to established curriculum

Requirements: 30 hours/week with split shift possible

Contract: Nine months

Qualifications: Native English speaker, B.A./B.S. degree plus one or more years of full-time ESL teaching experience or degree in TESL/TEFL

Preferences: Advanced degree in TESL/TEFL plus two years' ESL experience

Salary: 2,200 euro/month

Benefits: Round-trip airfare, medical coverage, paid vacation, sick leave, and onsite orientation

Attending National and Regional Conferences

TESOL holds an annual convention that is well attended (5,000+ TESOLers travel from afar to this yearly event) by teachers, program developers, and administrators, many of whom are also there to find employment—or employees. In fact, the annual TESOL convention is one of the best ways to secure an EFL job.

In addition to the various speakers, presentations, and other professional development opportunities the conference offers, TESOL maintains an onsite employment clearinghouse. Space is set aside each year where hiring institutions can post their job openings and study résumés of prospective candidates. Curtained booths are made available for face-to-face interviews that often result in on-the-spot job offers. A large number of seasoned EFL teachers can claim at least one position secured by this means.

TESOL affiliates (autonomous organizations with a separate membership from TESOL) also hold regional conferences throughout the United States at different times during the year and recruiters attend these events as well, although on a smaller scale than the annual convention. TESOL's central office will locate an affiliate contact near you.

NAFSA is another large organization with an annual convention that attracts job recruiters.

International Schools Services (ISS), an employment agency for teachers and related school personnel, is examined more fully in Chapter 5. It should be noted here, however, that every February and March, ISS sponsors two International Recruitment Centers (IRCs) in the United States and one overseas. During this time, overseas administrators make recruitment trips to fill their staffing needs. Approximately 550 teaching positions are listed at the IRCs each year. Active ISS candidates may register and schedule interviews with prospective employers. ISS places more than 350 teachers and administrators each year, and it reports that 70 percent of these candidates secure their positions at one of the IRCs.

Registering with EFL Employment Agencies

There are many private employment agencies that deal exclusively with teaching and related positions. As a job seeker you would usually be asked to fill out an application; provide several copies of your résumé, diplomas/credentials, and letters of reference; and state your preferred geographical locations. You will also be asked to pay a registration/service fee. When signing up with an agency, it is best to go with an organization whose reputation you are familiar with. There are many fly-by-night employment agencies to watch out for. Some of the warning signs are:

1. Their fees are usually exorbitant.
2. They insist you fly to their office at your own expense.
3. They inform you of just the right job opening and ask you to pay a deposit in "good faith" to hold the job for you.
4. They make unsubstantiated claims, such as promising a woman an EFL position in a private company in Saudi Arabia. (Women are restricted to only a few particular job settings in Saudi Arabia.)

Contacting Hiring Institutions Directly

Often institutions, particularly smaller ones overseas, do not always advertise their openings in the United States or through the other usual channels. If there is a particular country in which you hope to work, or a particular institution to which you would like to apply, it can be advantageous to make a direct approach.

At your library or on the Internet, you can find listings of domestic and overseas schools, universities, and language centers. For overseas institutions, you can also write or telephone a specific country's embassy in Washington, D.C., and ask for its educational/cultural affairs office. Often the officer in charge of that department also plays some role in the recruitment procedure and will know of any openings in his or her home country.

Networking

Word-of-mouth is still one of the most effective ways to learn of job openings, particularly in the TESOL profession. You can find other ESL/EFL teachers in your own program or at regional and national conventions. Talk to these other teachers and find out where they've worked and how to go about applying. Former or current employees of a particular institution can provide a wealth of information about employment and living conditions.

Traveling "On Spec"

Some more intrepid TESOLers have traveled to their location of choice with the hopes of finding employment upon arrival. In some countries, such as Japan or Spain, this can be a successful method, securing teaching on a part-time basis in local language schools or finding individual students to tutor privately. But it's a risky proposition. More and more language schools seek professional candidates through the normal channels, and if your travel and living expenses depend upon finding employment, you could find yourself a long way from home without funds.

There are also a few other disadvantages to this method. Many employers expecting to hire staff from the United States or United Kingdom also expect to pay for air tickets, accommodations, and other expenses such as baggage and settling-in allowances. By arriving unannounced on an employer's doorstep, you might be short-changing yourself an attractive salary and benefits package.

In addition, work visas in some countries can only be obtained when the candidate is outside the country. You could arrive, find a job, then discover that you have to leave again to satisfy work and immigration regulations. Finally, some countries will deny you entry unless you have a sponsor (an employer) in advance.

Searching Online

There are many websites with databases that allow you to search for EFL jobs in specific countries or by type of job setting.

For example, CompuServe operates the Foreign Language Forum, which advertises ESL/EFL and other language-related positions. The Foreign Language Forum is also a good way to communicate with other TESOLers to find out information about employment conditions in a variety of settings. It can be found at http://forums.compuserve.com/gvforums/default.asp?SRV=foreign language.

NAFSA, the Association of International Educators, also lists job openings on its website, nafsa.org.

TESOL, Inc. operates TESL-L, an electronic communications resource for anyone interested in the TESOL profession. You can get more information at hunter.cuny.edu/~tesl-l.

TESLK-12 is a new net for teachers of English as a second or foreign language in grades K–12. To participate on TESLK-12 send a message to listserv@cunynvm.cuny.edu with the message "SUBSCRIBE TESLK-12," or contact the TESOL office for more information.

Other sites include Teaching Jobs Overseas at nea.org/resources/freestuf/messages/62.html and overseasjobs.com/index.html, which is a newsletter and directory of resources that also lists job notices. Use any search engine to locate other databases listing job vacancies.

5

DEPARTMENT OF DEFENSE DEPENDENTS SCHOOLS AND INTERNATIONAL SCHOOLS

IN ADDITION TO EFL opportunities overseas as outlined in Chapter 4, classroom teachers and other school personnel find satisfying employment in Department of Defense Dependents Schools and a variety of international schools.

Department of Defense Dependents Schools

The Department of Defense Dependents Schools (DoDDS) is a worldwide school system operated by the Department of Defense (DOD) in 14 foreign countries. Its mission is to provide a quality education from prekindergarten through grade 12 for the eligible minor dependents of DOD military and civilian personnel on official overseas assignments.

Approximately 6,500 educators serve roughly 86,000 students in 167 elementary, middle, and secondary schools and one community college.

DoDDS is an organizational element of the Department of Defense Education Activity, a DOD Field Activity. From the Office of Dependents Education (ODE) in Arlington, Virginia, the director manages a unified school system with three area superintendents and 12 district offices.

The area superintendents' offices are located in Wiesbaden, Germany; Okinawa, Japan; and Arlington, Virginia. Area superintendents manage the area staff and supervise superintendents who oversee districts of approximately 2 to 24 schools administered by local school principals.

School facilities in the DoDDS system vary. Although the buildings differ, each school is held to the same high standards.

Schools are accredited by the North Central Association of Colleges and Schools (NCA), one of six accrediting associations in the United States. Junior high, middle, and elementary schools with an enrollment of 150 students or more and all high schools are accredited.

Schools with smaller enrollments are certified by the NCA, assuring parents that their children receive an excellent education comparable to that available in the United States.

DoDDS Programs

DoDDS is committed to providing a progressive, quality education for all students by maintaining pupil-to-teacher staffing ratios and school funding comparable to that found in the United States. An intensive staff development program is emphasized, and all areas of the academic and cocurricular programs receive the necessary resources to operate a world-class, quality educational system.

Every effort is made to satisfy or exceed the important standards embodied in the National Education Goals. DoDDS supports the concept that high expectations promote superior student achievement and vigorously communicates to students, parents, and educators the importance of high expectations to attain academic excellence.

Throughout the school system, programs and efforts promoting high expectations are identified and implemented. DoDDS is a leader in implementing programs directly aimed at achievement of National Education Goals. Some of the programs include: Advancement Via Individual Determination, Reading Recovery, Cooperative Integrated Reading and Composition, Families and Schools Together, Distance Education, National Council of Teachers of Mathematics Standards (NCTM), Systemwide Writing Assessment, Sure Start, DARE (Drug Abuse Resistance Education), Language Immersion, and staff development programs.

The curriculum in the overseas schools is patterned after the finest educational programs in the United States. Educational programs range from college preparatory courses to vocational career programs, with on-the-job training at military installations.

The range of special programs available in DoDDS includes special education, English as a second language, and talented and gifted programs. DoDDS ensures all students equal access to educational programs and services while accommodating all levels of scholastic achievement. Programs are continually evaluated and upgraded through leadership at all levels, self-evaluation, and community involvement.

Two Who Have Been There

Vern Liermann spent 31 years working for Department of Defense Dependents Schools. He was posted in different locations within

Spain and Germany and held a variety of positions ranging from classroom teacher to assistant principal. His students were children of U.S. servicemen and -women.

"Our workday was similar to what it was like in the United States. The school year and the school day were the same as stateside. What we were able to do outside the school day and the school year was the attraction. In the early days of our stay in Europe, most teachers spent each summer traveling in Europe—usually camping. Every two years the government returned us to our point of hire and we spent the summer in the United States. For us this was an attractive combination. We traveled extensively in Europe and were able to keep in touch with our family and friends at home.

"Our tours of duty were in Spain and Germany. In both places I thought that we were well received. We traveled within those countries during the school year and often ate out in local restaurants. It was a very comfortable situation. Our three children were born in Europe, in hospitals operated by the military. For most of the years, we were provided with excellent, low-cost medical care. We shopped in the PX, commissary, and on the local economy."

Vern describes his most recent position. "I was the assistant principal in a 600-student school (K through grade six). My biggest responsibility was as school disciplinarian. As such, I dealt directly with quite a few students and their parents. The military command was always very supportive in helping us deal with recalcitrant students or parents. In extreme cases the military member would be reassigned. I would spend the day observing classrooms, supervising the lunchroom, supervising the loading and unloading of the buses, and arranging for field trips. Annually we took the entire student body by train to a music production in Saarbrücken, Germany. It was a great life."

John P. Brokaw spent more than 30 years working with the Department of Defense Dependents Schools in France, Turkey, Japan, Korea, the Philippines, and Germany. He also held a wide range of positions in the DOD system, from music teacher to high school principal.

John says of his experience, "My job as a teacher in the DoDDS was very much like it would have been in any stateside school. My daily routine was the same as any other teacher. We became used to having students move in and out during the school year, because a three-year assignment was about the maximum for most students.

"As a high school band director, my weekends were often taken up with football games and other sporting events, just as in the States. People often ask what the schools and students are like in the DoDDS system. That is not an easy question to answer. It is like asking what kind of schools and students you have in any large metropolitan area. Just as you have areas with affluent parents who are well educated or areas where families have little formal education, the military communities vary in the same way.

John concludes, "Those seeking to work for the DoDDS system have great opportunities. Those who work in jobs that have no connection with the American community must be ready to make substantial adjustments to their way of life. But that is not necessarily a problem if one is flexible and can adjust. In fact, it can be exciting. But for those in education, the DoDDS opportunity is a good one."

DOD Application Requirements and Information

The minimum DOD eligibility and qualification requirements include the following:

1. Applicants must be U.S. citizens.
2. Applicants must have the physical ability to perform the duties efficiently and without hazard to self or others. Because medical care in some overseas areas is limited, applicants requiring medical care or treatment must ensure that such care or treatment is available at the overseas location for themselves and their family members. Although some military medical facilities may be available, applicants should expect to receive their medical care from the local economy. Those requiring accommodations for a disability should contact the Staffing Section.
3. Availability on a worldwide basis is required and applicants should be available for immediate processing as soon as an employment offer is made.
4. A bachelor's degree from an institution accredited by a regional accrediting association is required. Academic preparation of at least 40 semester hours (SH) in general education course work distributed over such fields as English, history, social studies, mathematics, fine arts, languages, science, philosophy, and psychology is required. In addition, a minimum of 18 SH of professional teacher education coursework in such areas as learning process, measurement, philosophy, psychology, social foundations, methods of teaching, and curriculum applicable to the type and level of the position for which applying is required. (Note: communications impaired teachers, school nurses, school psychologists, school social workers, JROTC instructors, and noncertified training instructors are excluded from the minimum academic preparation requirement.)
5. Student teaching or an internship as part of an approved teacher education program in an accredited U.S. institution is required. In the absence of an approved student teaching

or internship program, applicants may be given credit for one year of successful full-time employment as an educator. Since the one year of employment substitutes for a course, no credit may be given for pay purposes. (Note: communications impaired teachers, school nurses, guidance counselors, school psychologists, school social workers, JROTC instructors and noncertified training instructors are excluded from the student teaching requirement.)

6. Credits or degrees earned from a foreign college or university must be evaluated prior to acceptance. Three evaluation procedures are acceptable:

   • The work is evaluated and interpreted by the International Education Research Foundation, Inc., Credential Evaluation Service, P. O. Box 66940, Los Angeles, CA 90066.

   • The foreign institution that awarded the degree is on a list endorsed by a regionally accredited university or on a list endorsed by a state department of education for the purpose of teacher certification in that state. (This procedure will require an English translation of the transcript and a copy of the document awarding the degree, together with an authenticated list produced by an American university or a state department of education.)

   • The work is evaluated by the graduate division of a regionally accredited university and declared the equivalent of similar undergraduate or graduate work in a U.S. institution. Graduates of nonaccredited institutions may have their undergraduate work validated by admittance to graduate school and completion of a minimum of five SH of credit in a regionally accredited graduate college.

7. In lieu of meeting the DoDDS minimum qualifications, applicants may be considered and hired based on a valid

state or territory certificate or license in the subject area for which applying. Educators appointed based on state or territory certificates may be granted a provisional license. A professional license may be granted upon completion of all applicable qualification standards as stated in this brochure and two years of successful teaching experience with DoDDS.

8. DoDDS licensure. There are three types of licenses issued to DoDDS employees:

   • Emergency license. This license is issued only when a fully qualified, licensed applicant is not available for the position, and the position is essential to the instructional program. It is valid for one school year.

   • Provisional license. Newly hired educators (other than those who are issued an emergency license) will be issued a provisional license. The provisional license is valid for two school years. Requirements for the professional license must be completed no later than the second school year of employment.

   • Professional license. Educators who have completed two years of successful teaching experience with DoDDS and meet all qualification requirements will be issued a DoDEA professional license.

9. Applicants must submit proof of achieving DoDEA minimum scores for any required PRAXIS test(s).

10. In addition to meeting the academic requirements, most positions require participation in extracurricular activities.

11. Males born after December 31, 1959, must (subject to certain exceptions) be registered with the Selective Service System.

12. Interviews are normally scheduled in December and January in accordance with projected staffing needs. Those

applicants who are not interviewed will continue to receive consideration for vacant positions and, if needed, will be contacted at a later date to be interviewed. All expenses incurred with the interview are the responsibility of the applicant. Applicants may select their preferred interview site on the enclosed application checklist.

13. Applicants who will be locally available may submit their applications before traveling to the overseas area. However, upon arrival they are required to update the application immediately with new contact information and a list of the specific schools for which employment consideration is requested.

    Family member applicants receive preference in employment. A family member is a spouse or unmarried child (under 23 years of age) of a member of a uniformed service, a federal civilian employee, or a nonappropriated fund employee officially assigned to an overseas area. This preference is afforded only in the commuting area of the sponsor's duty station, and does not apply to family members of retired sponsors or U.S. employees of private firms. This preference does not ensure selection over nonfamily members who are otherwise better qualified. Candidates claiming family member preference must include a copy of the sponsor's orders with their applications.

14. Preference in hiring will be afforded to former members of the military services who meet the requirements for veterans' preference. Specific information regarding eligibility for veterans' preference is available from the Office of Personnel Management's website, opm.gov.

15. Individuals who are currently employed with DoDDS on permanent educator appointments are not eligible to apply. Former DoDDS employees who were on permanent

appointments must have a break in employment of at least one school year from the date of voluntary separation to be eligible for reappointment.

16. DoDDS employs the best-qualified professional staff to implement its program of learning. These special selection factors are applied to determine the best-qualified and suitable applicants:
    - Academic preparation
    - Information secured through employment references and sources
    - Recommendation from interviewer
    - Recent experience as an educator
    - Possession of personal qualifications and traits, such as stability and ability to adapt to unusual and sometimes stressful situations, which are essential for successful performance in an overseas assignment
    - Academic preparation to teach more than one subject or grade level (Note: this flexibility is critical to meet the needs of the ever-changing population of students.)
    - Special achievements or awards related to the position(s) for which being considered

17. While applications are accepted at any time, applicants are encouraged to apply by early January to be considered for the next school year.

DoDDS Program Benefits and General Information

The type of appointment and location of residence at the time of appointment determine eligibility for allowances, differentials, and transportation agreements. Those who are selected will be advised of their eligibility for allowances, transportation, and other benefits at the time an offer is extended.

Salary

Salaries are comparable to rates for similar positions in urban school jurisdictions in the United States having a population of 100,000 or more. Vern concurs: "The salary package compared very favorably with stateside school systems. Housing was provided above the salary."

Teachers are paid on seven different academic salary lanes (ASL) to credit degrees and graduate course work completed after each degree. The current ASLs are bachelor's degree, bachelor's plus 15 semester hours, bachelor's plus 30 semester hours, master's degree, master's plus 15 semester hours, master's plus 30 semester hours, and doctorate degree. Service increments or steps are provided to recognize years of verified experience up to a maximum. To access the most recent educator salary schedules, reference the DOD's compensation Web page at odedodea.edu/pers/classcomp.

John offers some firsthand insights on this issue, too. "The pay for DoDDS educators is set annually based on the average for large U.S. metropolitan school districts. That is set by law. One also gets housing in addition to the pay. Those who live on the military base receive free housing. Those who live on the local economy receive a housing allowance that can be used for rent and utilities. If you choose housing that costs more than the established allowance for the particular area, the additional cost must be born by you. But the addition of tax-free housing is a great benefit."

Health and Other Benefits

A voluntary health benefits program is available for eligible government employees. The government shares the cost of the plan.

For complete information about this program, reference the Federal Employees Health Benefits (FEHB) home page at opm.gov/insure.

A low-cost insurance plan with several options is available to eligible employees. The government shares the cost of the basic plan. For complete information about this program, reference the Federal Employees Group Life Insurance (FEGLI) home page at opm .gov/insure/life.

Eligible employees are covered by the Federal Employees' Retirement System (FERS). FERS is a three-part retirement plan consisting of Social Security Benefits, FERS basic benefits, and a Thrift Savings Plan (TSP). For complete information about FERS, see its website at opm.gov/retire. For complete information about TSP, see its website at.tsp.gov.

A living quarters allowance is paid to eligible employees by the U.S. government to help defray rental and utility charges when housing is rented on the local economy. Government housing may be provided in some overseas areas without charge. Unaccompanied personnel may be required to share government quarters. Extended stays in temporary housing may be necessary at some posts while awaiting suitable housing for the employee and family. Generally, only applicants recruited in the United States are eligible for a living quarters allowance.

Length of Assignment

Tours of duty are one or two school years depending on the area of assignment.

- One-year tour areas: Bahrain, Cuba, Iceland, Italy (Sigonella and La Maddalena), Korea, Japan (Misawa and Okinawa), Portugal (Azores), and Turkey.

- Two-year tour areas: Belgium, England, Germany, Italy (other than Sigonella and La Maddalena), Greece, Japan (other than Misawa and Okinawa), Netherlands, and Spain.

Transportation Agreement

Selected applicants must sign a transportation agreement to commit to remain overseas for the tour of duty. Transportation is provided for eligible employees, their family members, and household goods to and from the overseas area. Upon successful completion of a tour of duty, employees may commit to another tour of duty and be granted travel to and from the United States at government expense.

Selected applicants are also required to sign a mobility certificate indicating that they understand and agree to be reassigned to other school positions at any location within the DoDDS system for which they are determined qualified.

Shipment of Household Goods

Shipment and/or storage of household goods and personal effects are at government expense for eligible employees. The weight allowances vary according to location and will be determined at the time of processing.

Shipment of Automobile

The shipment of a privately owned automobile at government expense may be authorized in certain areas for eligible employees. There may be restrictions on model, size, year, and country of origin of the vehicle.

Shipment of Pets

The shipment and quarantine of pets are at the expense of the employee. These expenses can be quite high. Pets are not authorized entry into some areas. Some countries impose lengthy quarantines on pets.

Medical and Dental Facilities

Applicants should be prepared to use the medical and dental services of the host country. Military dispensaries are available to provide emergency services in some locations, but the nearest military hospital facilities may be located some distance away. If military facilities are available, a charge will be assessed for medical services. Applicants should determine whether adequate medical care is available in the country concerned prior to accepting an assignment if they or their family members have medical problems or require medication. Military dental clinics are usually only available to provide emergency services.

Special Education

The Department of Defense Dependents Schools provides education including special education to the children of DOD civilians who are eligible to attend a DoDDS school. Students must meet DoDDS criteria for special education. Services are provided based on an individualized educational program. Most schools are not staffed for all disabilities. The DoDDS staffs schools in specific locations for a full range of disabilities. Prior to accepting a position, applicants who have children with significant disabilities (i.e., blindness, deafness, severe mental retardation, and serious emotional impairments) should ensure that the child's educational need could be met at the location of the job. Applicants may review the special needs network for more specific information on the location of special education services overseas.

Position Categories

Elementary School Teacher Positions

Prekindergarten
Kindergarten
Kindergarten, language
  immersion
Elementary grades 1–3
Elementary grades 4–6
Elementary grades 7–8
Compensatory
  education, reading
Compensatory
  education,
  mathematics

Elementary grades 1–3,
  language immersion
Elementary grades 4–8,
  language immersion
Art
Music
Physical education
Reading recovery
  teacher
Reading recovery
  teacher leader

Middle School (Grades 6–8) Teacher Positions

English
Speech
Journalism
Social studies

General science
Health
Mathematics

Secondary School (Usually Grades 7–12) Teacher Positions

English
Speech
Journalism
Drama
Social studies
General science
Biology
Chemistry
Physics
Health
Mathematics
Art
Music
Humanities
Physical education
Business

Computer science
Industrial arts
Coordinator work
    experience
Driver education
Home economics
Technology education
French
German
Latin
Spanish
Japanese
Korean
Turkish
Italian
Dutch

Training Instructor (Vocational)

Automotive technology
Electronic technology
Cosmetology
Graphic arts
Welding
Dental technology
Medical technology
Small engine repair
Musical instrument
    repair

Computer technology
Fashion design
Power technology (solar,
    thermal, hydro, or
    nuclear)
Agriculture
Industrial equipment
    repair

Junior Reserve Officers Training Corps (JROTC) Instructor

Officer, Marine Corps	Officer, Air Force
NCO, Marine Corps	NCO, Air Force
Officer, Navy	Officer, Army
PO, Navy	NCO, Army

Pupil Personnel Services Positions

(* designates that separate positions exist at the elementary, middle, and secondary levels.)

Dormitory Counselor/Resident Hall Advisor	School social worker Educational prescriptionist*
School psychologist	Guidance counselor*

Educational Support Positions

(* designates that separate positions exist at the elementary, middle, and secondary levels.)

Language arts/reading specialist*
Speech/language pathologist assessor
Assessor (special education)
Teacher, severely learning impaired/multiple disabilities*
Teacher, physically impaired (grades pre-K–12)
Teacher, mildly to moderately learning impaired*
Teacher, moderately to severely learning impaired*
Teacher, emotionally impaired*
Teacher, preschool children (ages 3–5) with disabilities
Teacher, talented and gifted (TAG)*
Teacher, English as a second language (ESL)*
Teacher, compensatory education

Middle
Secondary
Teacher, hearing impaired (K–12)
Teacher, visually impaired (K–12)
Teacher, speech/language pathologist
School nurse
Information specialist*
School educational technologist
Career education coordinator

How to Apply

While applications for positions are accepted at any time, applicants are encouraged to apply by early January to be considered for the next school year. Applications for administrators come through the Educator Career Program and are accepted only when a specific opening has been announced.

For further information about DOD Dependents Schools opportunities and application forms, contact:

Department of Defense Dependents Schools (DoDDS)
ATTN: Teacher Recruitment
4040 North Fairfax Drive
Arlington, Virginia 22203-4634
odedodea.edu

International Schools

As mentioned in Chapter 4, the U.S. State Department through its Office of Overseas Schools maintains interest in some overseas international schools. Others are independent entities and can be contacted directly for employment possibilities. Addresses for a selected few international schools are supplied in Appendix C. Other addresses can be obtained by contacting the Washington, D.C., embassy of the country in which you would like to work. Some recruiters for international schools also attend the TESOL conference.

Teachers in international schools can be paid in U.S. dollars or in local currency. Housing and airfare are sometimes included.

Students attending international schools could be citizens of the host country or children of expatriate workers residing in the host country. International schools generally cover grades K through 12, although some schools go only through the end of middle school, and students entering high school must either return to their home countries or attend private boarding schools abroad.

Most international schools follow either a U.S. or U.K. curriculum and generally offer a high standard of education. Teachers are needed in all subject areas, and recruiters look for the same professionals found in DoDDS schools.

Many of the same avenues followed to secure an EFL teaching job overseas (as detailed in Chapter 4) can be followed to find work in international schools. Recruiters attend professional conferences and place vacancy notices in publications such as the *Chronicle of Higher Education* or with college placement offices.

You can access online databases listing openings in international schools via the Internet. Utilizing the services of reputable employment agencies also can lead to suitable placements. International Schools Services is one such agency.

International Schools Services

International Schools Services (ISS) is a private, not-for-profit organization founded in 1955 to support and advance the education of

American and other expatriate children attending school overseas. ISS headquarters is in Princeton, New Jersey, and is staffed by professional personnel experienced in international education.

ISS provides services to overseas schools including recruitment and recommendation of personnel, curricular and administrative guidance, school management, materials procurement, financial management, consulting services, and publications.

In addition to the International Recruitment Centers (mentioned in Chapter 4), services to job candidates include a year-round placement program for vacancies that occur in the late spring, summer, and mid-year.

The American and international schools using the ISS recruitment service are attended by a multinational student body of the children of international business and diplomatic personnel. Schools are located throughout Africa, Asia, Central and South America, Europe, and the Middle East. The language of instruction is English, and the curriculum follows a standard U.S. program. Because many of the children come from families where English is not the native language, opportunities also exist for EFL teachers.

ISS will accept candidates with at least a bachelor's degree and at least two years of current, successful, full-time elementary or secondary school experience. (The two-years' experience is sometimes waived in certain situations.) Although ISS does not require teaching certification, many of the schools that recruit through ISS do.

Because the number of applicants for administrative positions exceeds the number of available jobs, administrators with previous overseas work experience are in a better position to be offered jobs.

ISS applicants pay a modest registration fee that covers processing of the registration packet and review of the applicant's qualifications. A larger placement fee is charged when a candidate accepts a position secured through ISS efforts. Some schools will pay the placement fee for the candidate.

For more information and an application, write to:

International Schools Services
P.O. Box 5910
Princeton, New Jersey 08543
iss.edu

6

THE FOREIGN SERVICE

A CAREER SERVING your country overseas can offer excitement, challenge, and even glamour. As a member of the Foreign Service, which is under the jurisdiction of the United States Department of State, you can travel the world and, at the same time, gain the satisfaction of helping other people and representing the interests of your country.

Being a part of the Foreign Service is more than just a job. It is a complete way of life that requires dedication and commitment. If you're smart enough and tough enough to get the job done, the Foreign Service might just be the right place for you.

Positions Within the Foreign Service

The Foreign Service divides the different specialty areas into the following "cones":

Administration

Administrative personnel at overseas posts are responsible for hiring foreign national workers, providing office and residential space, ensuring reliable communications with Washington, D.C., supervising computer systems, and—of great importance in hostile or unfriendly areas—providing security for the post's personnel and property.

Consular Services

Consular workers must combine the skills of lawyers, judges, investigators, and social workers. Their duties range from issuing passports and visas to finding a lost child or helping a traveler in trouble.

Economic Officers

Economic officers maintain contact with key business and financial leaders in the host country and report to Washington on the local economic conditions and their impact on American trade and investment policies. They are concerned with issues such as commercial aviation safety, fishing rights, and international banking.

Political Affairs

Those working in political affairs analyze and report on the political views of the host country. They make contact with labor unions, humanitarian organizations, educators, and cultural leaders.

Information and Cultural Affairs

As part of the Foreign Service, the United States Information Agency (USIA) promotes U.S. cultural, informational, and public diplomacy programs. An information officer might develop a library available to the public, meet with the press, and oversee English language training programs for the host country.

Commercial and Business Services

In this division a Foreign Service officer identifies overseas business connections for American exporters and investors, conducts market research for the success of U.S. products, and organizes trade shows and other promotional events.

What It's Like Being a Foreign Service Officer

Foreign Service officers can be based in Washington, D.C., or can be sent anywhere in the world. They work at embassies, consulates, and other diplomatic missions in major cities or small towns. They help the thousands of Americans traveling and living overseas, issue visas to citizens of other countries wishing to visit the United States, and help our government execute our foreign policies.

The Foreign Service officer accepts direction from the President of the United States and his top appointees. The main goal is to make U.S. policies succeed. He or she is expected to place loyalty over personal opinions and preferences.

Upsides and Downsides

Foreign Service workers can experience a glamorous lifestyle— dining with their ambassador in a European palace or meeting royalty or other heads of state, for example. They can be present at important decision-making sessions and influence world politics and history.

But postings can offer hardship as well, especially if they are in environments as hostile as Antarctica or as hot and dry as a Middle Eastern desert. Some assignments are in isolated locations without all the familiar comforts of home. The weather can be harsh, and there can be health hazards. Danger from unrest or war is always possible.

In spite of the difficulties, those in the Foreign Service are happy with the unique rewards and opportunities.

Insights of Three Veterans

These individuals have made Foreign Service a career. What they have to say will give you valuable insight into what the job is like.

Jim Van Laningham, General Services Officer

Jim Van Laningham has made the Foreign Service his career for more than 15 years. He's been posted in Russia, Poland, Morocco, Iraq, Washington, D.C., and Pakistan. He is a general service officer, which falls under the administration cone.

What It's Really Like

"An administrative officer is the person responsible for keeping the embassy operating on a day-to-day basis. First thing in the morning I might find a series of cables from Washington waiting for me, which would require me to report on certain information. Depending on the time of the year, I may be involved in renewing leases on houses we rent for our American staff or I may be involved in preparing the budget for the embassy, which could be anywhere from a million dollars and up. The budget covers salaries of embassy staff, electricity and other utilities, and the procurement of paper, pencils, computers, copy machines, and other office equipment.

"For lunch I may meet with several of my counterparts from Australian or Canadian or British embassies to discuss issues.

"Later in the day I may be involved in some personnel issues, where I evaluate employee performance and recommend promotion. Or I may have a discipline problem with an employee and have to talk to him or her about it. I'm even responsible for having to fire someone, if necessary.

"Entertaining is a big part of a Foreign Service officer's life, either having local people or people from other embassies to dinner, or going to dinner at someone else's home. Oftentimes you learn a lot about what's going on in the country from talking to other diplomats or the people who live there.

"On weekends you can travel around the country or go to other cities and see what there is to see. Not only just to play tourist, but to meet other people and talk to them."

The Upsides

"What I like most about being an administrative officer in the Foreign Service is the opportunity to see a problem, determine what the solution is, and then see it through to the end. Obviously travel is also a very attractive part of the job. You can live overseas in a country for a number of years and really get to know what it's like.

"And for me there's a lot of excitement about being able to represent the United States overseas—meeting important people in the country where you are living and, perhaps, even affecting how relations develop between the United States and that country.

"Another benefit working with the Foreign Service is that you can retire at age 50 after 20 years of service."

Solid Advice

"You have to be able to write well, to organize thoughts logically and coherently. You have to be outgoing because you deal with a lot of different people and you have to have people skills. I think you have to be interested in the world and what's going on around you, because a lot of what you do is reporting back to Washington on what's happening in the country you're in.

"And if you're in the administration cone, hopefully you are a good manager of people. You have to have leadership ability. It also helps to be familiar with finances and budgets.

"But I don't think there's any one particular field of study that leads to the Foreign Service. The people I've met have taken every imaginable major in school. It's more just studying well and doing well and getting a well-rounded education."

Robert Manzanares, Administrative Officer

Bob Manzanares entered the Foreign Service in 1978. He has held a variety of positions including consular officer, general services officer, chief of post management for the Middle Eastern bureau, and director for the office of administration for the National Security Council.

He has been posted in the Ivory Coast, West Africa, Mexico City, Iceland, Israel, and Washington, D.C.

What It's Really Like

"I was a consular officer in Mexico City, which was known as a 'visa mill.' Everyone wanted to come to the United States, and by eight o'clock in the morning we would have between two and three thousand people waiting in this huge line to enter the compound and apply for a visa. I was one of 14 officers working in a little *casita*, a makeshift hut, and we would listen to each applicant for a minute to a minute and a half and make a decision whether to issue a visa. This would go on nonstop from eight to two, and we would process more than 4,000 applications a day.

"In the afternoon we would issue visas with passports that came in through a tourist agency. It was the same work, but not as interesting because we didn't get to talk to the people.

"I also made prison visits. Occasionally, we'd have Americans who wound up in prison, for whatever reasons, and so my job was to go in and make sure they were not being abused and that they had access to an attorney.

"Also, if an American should die overseas, the consular officer has to contact the family and make arrangements to ship the body home.

"When I was with the Middle Eastern bureau in Washington, I was one of the main organizers, from the logistical side, of the Middle East Peace Talks that took place in Madrid. Working with a team, I helped organize the conference site and coordinated all the different arrangements that go into putting together a conference like that, from security, to transportation, to hotels, to interpreters—the whole gamut."

The Upsides and Downsides

"I like the flexibility of being able to change jobs and locations every so often. Before I joined the Foreign Service, I worked for six years in city administration. That was fun, but I couldn't see myself doing that for 20 years.

"The most difficult aspect of working in the Foreign Service is leaving behind all the people you've met. For the short period of time you're posted in a country, you get to know people there, they become your friends, your new family during holidays, and then you move on to the next post, and it's easy to lose touch."

Solid Advice

"Get a liberal arts background if you can, and have some experience before you try to get in. There's a lot of what I call trench time; it's a structured bureaucracy and you have to go through the steps to get to the top. Those people who come in with a little more life experience, not necessarily just work experience, fare better.

"It's a competitive service all the way around. There's competition for promotions; there's competition for different postings. It keeps you on your toes.

"You have to like people and be willing to accept and live among other cultures. There are inconveniences, but you should be flexible and not expect to transplant America with you when you go overseas."

Shirley Panasuk, Nurse

Shirley has worked as a nurse in U.S. embassies in a range of exotic places including Moscow, Baghdad, and Ankara, Turkey.

What It's Really Like

"There are two types of nurses who work in the Foreign Service: nurse practitioners and contract nurses. I am a contract nurse for the Department of State in a position they call 'PIT.' That stands for part-time, intermittent, temporary. My patients are the diplomats working in the U.S. embassy and their dependents.

"The job is always challenging, and it's always different. Nursing overseas we had to deal with almost every specialty: pediatrics, maternity, gynecology, any problem that you could think of. In fact, we dealt with even more interesting things because when you're living in a foreign country you can pick up unusual ailments such as parasites or stomach problems from eating the local food.

"I also had a lot of administrative work—ordering medications and making sure we had equipment and enough supplies in the office.

"We really had our hands in a lot of things. We had to read more and study so we knew what we were dealing with."

The Upsides

"As a nurse in the Foreign Service there's a sense of being needed, being wanted. You're very important to many people. While that's not the most important aspect of nursing, it is rewarding to be needed.

"And it's also rewarding when you have patients who are ill and frightened. You spend a lot of time with them and when they're finally better, they'll come back to thank you.

"I chose this profession because I wanted to help people, and there is nothing I would like to do more than be a nurse."

Salaries and Benefits

Salaries follow the government pay scale. The starting salary is generally low, but it may be increased at overseas posts with free housing, furniture and utilities, travel expenses, educational allowances for children, and cost-of-living allowances in high-cost cities. Extra pay is also given for dangerous and "hardship" posts.

At current pay rates, new Foreign Service officers earn a basic annual salary of between $26,708 and $43,874, depending upon experience. All candidates except those with additional experience as described below start at $26,708.

Candidates with a bachelor's degree or a combination of five years' university education and full-time professional experience in a field similar to or closely related to the work of the Foreign Service start at $30,000.

Candidates with a master's degree, law degree, or a combination of seven years' university education and full-time professional experience in a field similar to or closely related to the work of the Foreign Service begin at $33,600.

Candidates with a doctorate or successful completion of all requirements for a doctorate except for the dissertation, or a combination of nine years' university education and full-time professional experience in a field similar to or closely related to the work of the Foreign Service begin at $35,600.

Newly hired Foreign Service officers with foreign language skills may qualify for additional salary at entry. Within 30 days of entering the Foreign Service, new officers who claim proficiency in foreign languages can be tested at the Language Testing Unit of the National Foreign Affairs Training Center. Hires who demonstrate a specific level of professional competency in one or more foreign languages can receive pay increases of up to several thousand dollars.

In some cases the Foreign Service matches the salary of officers transferring from civilian federal agencies. In extraordinary cases, the United States Information Agency may offer starting salaries at a higher rate than those listed above.

Salary Ranges

There are three career stages in the Foreign Service. Their annual salary range is presented below.

Career Stage	Annual Salary Range
Junior Officer	$26,708–$43,874
Career Officer	$45,000–$90,000
Senior Foreign Service	$93,000–$116,000

Health Insurance

Foreign Service officers and their families are eligible for health insurance coverage starting with the date of employment. A variety of health insurance options are available to officers, including fee-for-service plans and HMOs. The employee covers a portion of the cost, and this is paid through payroll deductions.

Other Benefits

Other benefits available to Foreign Service officers include a life insurance plan and a variety of retirement benefits, such as annuity programs, investment and savings programs, pension plans, social security benefits, Medicare coverage, and additional retirement income.

Getting Started

Although many Foreign Service officers are skilled in political science and history, these days candidates can have knowledge in specialized fields such as the environment, computer science, the fight against AIDS, antidrug efforts, and trade.

There are several steps to complete to apply for a position in the Foreign Service:

- **Written Examination.** This is a daylong multiple-choice test usually given once a year. It measures verbal and numerical reasoning, political and cultural awareness, English-language expression, and knowledge of topics important to the function of the Foreign Service. It's a difficult exam, and many people have to take it more than once before they pass.

- **Oral Evaluation.** Those who pass the written exam will be invited to participate in an all-day oral assessment. This test measures the skills, abilities, knowledge, and personal characteristics necessary to succeed in the Foreign Service. Writing skills are also measured, as well as administrative, problem-solving, leadership, and interpersonal skills.
- **Medical Clearance.** Because many postings have inadequate health care or pose health hazards, candidates for the Foreign Service must meet a high medical standard. However, allowances are made for certain handicaps.
- **Background Investigation.** The Department of State, along with other federal, state, and local agencies, conducts a thorough background check on Foreign Service candidates. They examine employment records, credit history, repayment of school loans, drug abuse, and criminal records.

Eligibility

Before you can take the Foreign Service written examination you must be:

- At least 20 years of age on the date of the exam
- No older than 59 years of age
- A citizen of the United States
- Available for worldwide assignment

Job Outlook

The Foreign Service exam is not always offered on a yearly basis; the exam is given when there are definite positions to fill. Because competition is keen for all positions with the Foreign Service, the number of candidates tends always to exceed the number of openings. Most openings arise from the need to replace Foreign Service workers who retire or leave the profession for other reasons.

How to Apply

For information on the Foreign Service exam and how to apply for the Foreign Service, contact:

Department of State
Recruitment Division
P.O. Box 9317
Rosslyn Station
Arlington, Virginia 22091
careers.state.gov

7

THE PEACE CORPS

THE PEACE CORPS is a U.S. government agency that sends more than 6,600 U.S. citizens abroad every year to assist countries that have requested its help. Although most people are aware of the Peace Corps as a volunteer organization, many don't realize that it takes a number of paid staff to run operations. The Peace Corps hires more than 800 people to work in the United States and to manage volunteer programs in approximately 69 countries overseas.

In this chapter you will learn about both paid and volunteer opportunities with the Peace Corps.

Paid Peace Corps Positions

Peace Corps volunteers are supported by a staff of salaried employees that includes more than 800 U.S. citizens worldwide. Of these, most employees work at Peace Corps headquarters in Washington, D.C. Others work in the 11 regional offices that conduct recruiting events throughout the United States, and still others make up the Peace Corps' field staffs, who are posted in approximately 90 countries.

In one sense, Peace Corps positions are like many others found throughout government and across corporate America. The Peace Corps employs accountants, managers, administrative assistants, recruiters, computer programmers, overseas program directors, country directors, medical officers, and a variety of other professionals to staff its offices.

There are several types of international positions within the Peace Corps. The most common are Associate Peace Corps Director (APCD) positions. On average, 30 American APCDs are hired per year. Of those, roughly half are posted in Africa and the remaining are posted in other areas, such as the Asia-Pacific region, Europe, Central Asia, the Mediterranean region, and the Inter-America region.

APCD positions include the following:

APCD Administration

These APCDs provide technical advice and guidance to the country director and supervise staff in all areas of administrative management. They are responsible for budget formulation and execution, personnel, procurement, property, and general services to the post. They are also responsible for the fiscal integrity of the country program and work closely with embassy personnel.

APCD Programming and Training

These APCDs administer Peace Corps programs for the host country and provide technical assistance and guidance to overseas staff in the development, management, and evaluation of project and training designs. They are responsible for general program development and all training and are sometimes second-in-charge at the post after the country director.

APCD Generalist

These APCDs generally are found in both large and small Peace Corps country programs. In the larger programs they usually function as regional directors for the Peace Corps, overseeing volunteers in many programmatic areas while living in those regions. In small programs they may handle the same programmatic and supervisory responsibilities as the larger program generalists, but their responsibilities will be nationwide, and they often will reside in the capital city. They are responsible for coordinating, implementing, and evaluating country-specific programs, which may cover two or more of the APCD programming sectors. The title of generalist is misleading because these APCDs need to be specialized in more than one field to qualify.

APCD Programming

These APCDs run programs in education, youth outreach, and community development; business development; environment; agriculture; health and HIV/AIDS; and information technology. Programming APCDs identify, develop, and support projects that reflect and serve the development needs of the country. They are responsible for refining existing projects as well as searching for new projects. The agriculture, environment, and business development APCDs coordinate with institutions such as nongovernmental organizations, financial institutions, and government agencies that support the development of their specific sectors. The education APCDs work with different types of educational institutions. Health APCDs focus on prevention, human capacity building, and education, working at the grassroots level where their impact can be the most significant and where health needs are most pressing.

Qualifications for APCD Positions

As the Peace Corps moves into its 36th year of service, several posts are increasing the number of host country nationals serving in APCD positions. This means that the vacancies available are becoming more and more competitive. Minimum qualifications that are listed in the vacancy announcements are rarely enough to get selected. Competitive candidates usually will have a master's degree, several years of managerial and counseling experience, technical skills, and fluency in the host country's language (especially in Spanish-speaking and Francophone countries).

In addition to APCD positions, there are two other categories:

Peace Corps Medical Officers

PCMOs provide health care to volunteers and staff overseas. Applicants for these positions must be medical doctors, osteopathic doctors, registered nurses, nurse practitioners, or physician assistants.

Country Directors (CD)

The CD is the senior agency official in country and is responsible for the overall management and direction of all aspects of the Peace Corps program. Individual programs differ considerably; programs range in size from approximately 20 volunteers to nearly 200, with annual operating budgets ranging from several hundred thousand dollars to roughly three million dollars.

CD candidates should have a background of demonstrated excellence in managing a program or business of comparable size to a

Peace Corps post. All CD applications are handled through the director's office.

Citizenship

Only citizens of the United States may be hired for Peace Corps jobs in the United States and for the country director, associate Peace Corps director, and staff Peace Corps medical officer jobs overseas. However, the Peace Corps does employ citizens of its host countries and other foreign nationals in both professional and support positions overseas. Foreign nationals seeking employment with the Peace Corps should direct their applications to the Peace Corps country director in the country in which they live.

All applications for jobs with the Peace Corps must specify the applicant's country of citizenship.

Time Limits on Peace Corps Employment

Appointments to work for the Peace Corps are limited to five years. Peace Corps employees are hired for an initial 30-month tour of duty and may be extended for another 30 months. After 60 months, employees must leave Peace Corps employment, unless their appointments are extended under special circumstances. This time limit is referred to as the "five-year rule." It was established to ensure that Peace Corps' staff members remain as fresh and innovative as its volunteers do.

Former Peace Corps employees cannot be reemployed by the Peace Corps until they have been out of the agency's employment for the same amount of time that they worked for the Peace Corps. For example, if you previously worked for the Peace Corps for three years, you cannot come back to work for the Peace Corps until you have been out of the agency's employment for three years. Service as a Peace Corps volunteer overseas is not counted for the purposes of this rule.

Language Requirements

Some positions require fluency in French, Spanish, or Portuguese. Other languages may be required according to the needs of the post. Applicants will be screened for language proficiency during the interview process and tested, within one month of entrance on duty, at the National Foreign Affairs Training Center.

Clearances

Selected candidates receive a conditional employment offer, pending medical and security clearances. The employee and any dependents must be medically cleared before overseas travel is authorized. Likewise a critical-sensitive security clearance for the employee must be granted before travel is authorized overseas. Failure to achieve either medical or security clearance normally results in revocation of the offer of employment.

Individuals who have been associated with certain intelligence activities cannot be considered for any vacancy. With your application packet you will be supplied with an intelligence background questionnaire to fill out.

Intangible Benefits

The Peace Corps' slogan is "The Toughest Job You'll Ever Love." With that in mind, the Peace Corps offers a challenging work environment. Peace Corps employees have to deal with unique problems that often directly affect the lives of other people. Whether you are determining the best way to combat malnutrition in South America or are faced with the task of providing Internet access to volunteers in Northern Africa, you will be forced to rise to the occasion and perform in a way you never thought possible.

Your coworkers will be a part of your "benefits package." The Peace Corps strives to hire the best possible individuals. Many of its employees have advanced degrees in specialized areas, others have significant overseas experience, and a large percentage is made up of volunteers returning to the Peace Corps.

Another plus to the work is that Peace Corps employees have the luxury of gaining exposure to the international arena regardless of where they are stationed. The day-to-day issues that confront Peace Corps staff are not unlike those common to people working in other international organizations.

Another Peace Corps slogan is a chance to "make a real difference." Since its inception, the Peace Corps has had a substantial impact on the lives of a large number of people in many developing nations. When you work for the Peace Corps, you have the satisfaction of knowing that you are making your own contribution to the work volunteers are doing around the world.

Tangible Benefits

The Peace Corps offers the benefits of federal employment. New staff members receive 13 vacation days (extended to four weeks after just three years of service), 11 federal holidays, 13 days of sick leave annually, a wide choice of life and health insurance plans, and a retirement system with a completely portable tax-deferred savings plan.

Salary

Salaries at the Peace Corps conform to government-wide ranges approved each year by Congress. If an application is selected, assignment of grade level will be based on work experience and education. Experience requirements must be met within 30 days after the Peace Corps receives the application.

Employees may enroll in one of several health plans offered to federal employees. The cost is shared by the government and no physical examination is required.

Low-cost life insurance is available. Like health insurance, the cost is shared by the government and no physical examination is required.

New employees are automatically enrolled in a three-tier system that includes Social Security, a basic pension plan, and a thrift savings plan. Under the thrift savings plan, employees may contribute up to 10 percent of basic pay into a tax-deferred interest account. The government will match the employee's contribution, up to 5 percent of basic pay.

Housing at post is provided by the Peace Corps, or the employee receives a housing allowance. Reasonable relocation expenses will be paid by the Peace Corps, unless the employee fails to complete the scheduled overseas tour for reasons within his or her control.

Applying for a Paid Peace Corps Position

To apply for any paid Peace Corps position, you must send the application materials described below and specify the vacancy number of the job you are applying for. The vacancy number always begins with PC, as in PC7–001, and is provided with the job opening announcement. You must submit a separate, complete application for each job for which you wish to be considered. Do not send a general application asking to be considered for all appropriate positions.

What Your Application Should Contain

You may apply for most jobs with a résumé, the Optional Application for Federal Employment (OF-612), the Standard Form 171, or any other written form you choose. Although the federal government does not require a standard application form for most jobs, certain information is needed to evaluate your qualifications. If you decide to submit any format other than the OF-612, (i.e., a résumé), the following information must be included:

1. Vacancy announcement number and position title.
2. A completed form PC-1336 (intelligence background information sheet). You can obtain this form by calling the Peace Corps job line at (800) 818-9579 and have a copy faxed or mailed to you.
3. A statement of U.S. citizenship (or of other citizenship if you are a foreign national applying for employment at a Peace Corps country office overseas). Completing OPM forms 1386 (background survey questionnaire) and 256 (self-identification of handicap) is strictly voluntary. All applicants will receive consideration regardless of race, color, religion, sex, national origin, age, disability, or political affiliation.
4. Name, address, and home and work phone numbers.
5. Social Security number.
6. If applicable, highest federal civilian grade held, job series, and date of last promotion.

7. High schools and universities attended. Please include school name, city, and state, and type and year of any degrees/diplomas you have received, as well as your major(s). If no degree, show total credit hours earned and indicate whether they are semester or quarter hours.
8. Relevant work experience (paid and unpaid). Include job title (with series and grade if federal), duties and accomplishments, employers' names and addresses, supervisors' names and phone numbers, hours worked per week if part-time, starting and ending dates of employment (month and year), and salary. Also indicate if the Peace Corps may contact your current supervisor.
9. Job-related training courses (titles and dates), skills (foreign languages, computer knowledge, typing speed, and so forth), and job-related certificates, licenses, honors, and special accomplishments. Qualifying work experience may be in the public or private sector. Education and experience may be combined to meet the minimum qualifications. (Applicants may not use postage-free government envelopes to submit applications. This is a violation of the law.)

Further information can be obtained at peacecorps.gov. Click on the "Jobs" link. The Peace Corps prefers applications to be submitted online.

Suggestions for Submitting a Successful Application

The Peace Corps receives many more applications than jobs it has to offer. The staffing process is extremely competitive, and many well-qualified applicants are not offered jobs. It is therefore crucial that your application specifically address the qualifications of the position in question. Each applicant is strongly encouraged to respond to each of the mandatory as well as the desired qualifications listed on the vacancy announcement. This may be done on a separate page attached to the résumé or other materials. The mandatory qualifications must be met to merit consideration for a job. No exceptions will be made.

Once an applicant is found qualified for a position, he or she will be further evaluated on the desired qualifications. These will be considered to determine which applicants are best qualified. Interviews and selections will be made for the best-qualified applicants.

It is critical that your application contain all the information you believe is pertinent in meeting the job qualifications. It is also critical that you file a job application for each job you are interested in with the Peace Corps. The Peace Corps cannot accept résumés and applications that do not reference a specific vacancy announcement. Applications outside of the opening and closing dates of a vacancy announcement also will not be accepted.

What to Expect After You Apply

As it arrives, each application is logged and entered into a database according to the vacancy number. A letter of acknowledgment is sent to the applicant. From that time the progress of the application is tracked in the database.

As soon as a vacancy closes (see the closing date on the vacancy announcement), all of the applications for that vacancy are reviewed as to whether they satisfy the basic requirements of the position specified in the vacancy announcement. Those that qualify are listed on a roster, which is then used as the pool from which the hiring department chooses candidates for interviews.

A period of interviews follows. Its length is at the discretion of the hiring department, as is the final decision regarding whom to hire. In any event, it may take up to three months to make a final selection for a particular job.

When the new employee is selected, all applicants are notified that a selection has been made.

Once you have submitted your application and it has been received and logged, you can be satisfied that you have done everything possible to promote your candidacy for the position. The hiring department may decide to contact you for an interview. However, because of the volume of applications received, many applicants are not interviewed.

Volunteering with the Peace Corps

When President John F. Kennedy delivered his inaugural address more than 40 years ago, he issued a call to service to Americans with the words, "Ask not what your country can do for you, ask what you can do for your country."

He manifested this vision by creating the Peace Corps, formed to promote world peace and mutual understanding and to offer trained men and women to countries in need.

Today's Peace Corps is as vital as ever, stepping into new countries like East Timor, and committing more than 1,000 new volunteers as a part of the HIV/AIDS Act of 2003 to work on HIV/AIDS prevention and education. The Peace Corps has intensified its role in the global effort to fight HIV/AIDS by training all volunteers in Africa as educators and advocates of HIV/AIDS prevention and education. Regardless of their primary project, all volunteers will be equipped to play a role in addressing the multiple health, social, and economic problems related to the HIV/AIDS epidemic. Peace

Corps programs in Botswana, Swaziland, and the Caribbean focus primarily on fighting the disease.

What Peace Corps Volunteers Do

Peace Corps volunteers have been fighting hunger, disease, illiteracy, poverty, and lack of opportunity around the world since 1961. Thanks to the efforts of more than 170,000 volunteers, over two and a half million acres of cropland are more productive; more than 14 million people have benefited from water, sanitation, and health programs; at least five million people have learned English, the international language of commerce; and thousands of new small businesses have been launched.

Peace Corps programs have evolved as the world has changed. While the need has remained for volunteers to work in agriculture, education, forestry, health, engineering, and skilled trades, countries are increasingly requesting help in new areas: business development, HIV/AIDS prevention and education, the environment, urban planning, youth development, and the teaching of English for commerce and technology.

Emerging democracies such as those of the former Soviet republics have turned to the Peace Corps for assistance for the first time, while previous Peace Corps hosts such as Chile and Ethiopia have reestablished relationships to address more advanced development issues.

International Opportunities in Education

Are you an experienced teacher? Are you a recent college graduate with a degree in an education field? Do you have certification to teach in a classroom? Do you want to experience teaching in another country? Have you been trained as a TEFL tutor? Do you have a degree in mathematics, science, or industrial arts? Do you enjoy sharing your skills with others?

Assignments are available all over the world. Depending on your qualifications, you might serve as a math teacher in Africa, primary teacher-trainer in the Caribbean, English teacher at a university in one of the former Soviet republics, or science teacher-trainer in Asia. Currently about 32 percent of Peace Corps volunteers work in the area of education, the single largest program component.

International Opportunities in Health and HIV/AIDS

Are you an experienced clinical professional in a health-related field? Are you a recent college graduate with a degree in health education, nursing, occupational or physical therapy, nutrition, or another health-related field? Do you have a college degree in biology or chemistry? Have you done volunteer work or been an educator in a health-related field? Are you interested in a career in international health?

Peace Corps volunteers help developing nations provide preventive health care to those most in need (such as women and children) and promote the development of health services to meet the local community's basic health needs. Currently about 20 percent of Peace Corps volunteers work in health programs. Forty-three countries benefit from the maternal and child health, health education and awareness, disease control, nursing education, water and sanitation, occupational and physical therapy, and HIV/AIDS education programs these volunteers offer.

International Opportunities in Environmental Fields

Do you have experience in environmental education, forestry park and wildlife management and interpretation, grant writing for environmental organizations, or environmental policy development? Do you have a bachelor's degree in forestry or national resources; environmental science, studies, or education; biology, botany, or geology; or wildlife biology? Are you certified to teach primary or secondary school science? Have you worked for at least six months in farming, forestry, 4-H, gardening, nurseries, or general construction? Have you been an extension agent or active in community tree planting or clean-up activities? Do you have a bachelor's degree in civil, structural, sanitary, or environmental engineering?

For more than 30 years, the Peace Corps has helped improve the environment by promoting environmentally sustainable development projects. Environmental programs are among the fastest growing in the Peace Corps, with 18 percent of volunteers working on these projects. From forestry to national parks to education, more than 1,000 Peace Corps volunteers working on environmental projects in 47 countries form one of the largest environmental workforces of any international development organization today.

Assignments are available all over the world. The specific skills required for each position vary, but Peace Corps environment projects generally fall into the following categories: agroforestry, forestry, environmental/forestry education, environmental organizational development, national parks/biological diversity, wildlife management, and water and sanitation engineering.

International Opportunities in Business Development

Are you an experienced businessperson? Are you a recent college graduate with a business degree? Do you have experience in marketing, banking, corporate finance, or accounting? Have you owned or managed a small- or medium-sized business? Do you have nonprofit management or public administration experience? Do you want business experience in a challenging new environment? Are you an entrepreneur at heart?

Market economies are catching on in places no one would have expected just a few years ago. In Latin America and Africa, small businesses are launched every day. Helping the local people get these ventures up and running is what 15 percent of Peace Corps volunteers focus their efforts on. All over the world, Peace Corps volunteers are helping businesses to develop.

Besides business savvy, you will need flexibility, commitment, and an inclination to do something different.

International Opportunities in Agriculture

Are you a recent college graduate in an agriculture-related field? Are you an experienced farmer or rancher? Have you worked in agribusiness? Are you interested in international agriculture? Did you major in biology, fisheries, or botany? Do you have at least six months' experience in farming, gardening, or nursery work?

As someone with an agriculture background, you have the knowledge and practical experience that are in demand in many developing countries. You might qualify for a volunteer assignment introducing farmers to new ways of improving the quality and quantity of their crops, teaching basic agricultural principles to students, or helping others start their own business.

Currently 7 percent of Peace Corps volunteers work in the area of agriculture and use their expertise to improve people's ability to produce food. Individuals with agriculture degrees, extensive farm or gardening experience (at least 18 months), or agribusiness backgrounds are sought for two-year volunteer assignments overseas.

Other Areas

The Peace Corps also has active programs in forestry, information technology, mathematics, science, engineering, skilled trades, and TEFL.

Volunteers provide technical training and support to groups and organizations that want to make better use of information and communications technology. They introduce people to the computer as a tool to increase efficiency and communication and to "leapfrog" stages of development. Volunteers teach basic computer literacy skills, e.g., word-processing, spreadsheets, basic accounting software, Internet use, and Web page development, and they introduce host communities to e-commerce, distance learning, and geographic information systems.

Peace Corps' TEFL projects generally fall into the following categories: secondary school teaching, teacher training, curriculum development, and university English teaching. For more information on TEFL jobs overseas, refer to Chapter 4.

One Volunteer's Experience

Angela Rekowski was posted in Mariakani, Kenya, from 1994 to 1996. She has a B.S. in mathematics with a teacher certification from Armstrong State College in Savannah, Georgia, and one year of graduate work in statistics toward her master's degree at the University of South Carolina.

"I taught math and a little physics in a secondary school in Mariakani, Kenya—about 40 kilometers west of Mombasa on the coast. It was very hot and humid for a lot of the year. Half the year is comfortable weather, half the year is unbearable.

"It's a very poor area compared to some of the schools other volunteers were placed at. We had one class at each grade level—between 25 and 50 students per class. Three of the classrooms had no doors or windows, and most of the time the school lacked things such as chalk, paper, books, and enough desks.

"Those kids have nothing, but most try really hard to succeed. Of course, there are the slackers who don't even try and the girls who are there just to increase their bride price. But most were fantastic and would have done anything for me if I'd asked them to."

Angela points out that there was no electricity—either in her house or in the school. Continuing, she says, "Then there are all the illnesses you can contract. Hot showers are few and far between, and washing all your laundry by hand isn't a bed of roses, especially when you're doing towels and sheets!

"My housing was provided by the school. I was fortunate that I had my own house. Other friends lived in compounds with many other people, and one girl lived with a family for two years. We were given a monthly stipend of about $200 in local currency to pay for food and other things of that nature.

"Medical was all taken care of. They gave you plenty of medical supplies, mosquito nets, and things such as a bike, if you needed one at your site.

"At the end of service, you have also accrued $200 per month while you were there. I left Kenya with about $5,200. You don't get that money until you leave though, and part of it is sent home.

"You go thinking you can make magnificent changes and reform, but you can't and you won't. You can't change tradition and culture in two years. You will, however, make a dent in a few lives, and those kids will remember you forever. They will be the ones to go on and make the changes.

"You'll make some of the best friends you've ever had and memories to last a lifetime."

Applying for a Volunteer Peace Corps Position

Applying to the Peace Corps can be exciting, but it can also be challenging. The application process involves essays, letters of recommendation, medical examinations, and interviews. You can get more information at peacecorps.gov.

The Peace Corps also operates 11 regional offices across the United States (Atlanta, Boston, Chicago, Dallas, Denver, Los Angeles, Minneapolis, New York, San Francisco, Seattle, and Washington, D.C.) that you can visit in person to ask questions and get the process started. In addition to assisting applicants, the regional offices conduct Peace Corps awareness programs and events, most frequently on college campuses.

The Application Process

After you submit your application to an area recruitment office, you will be sent a letter confirming its receipt. A recruiter assigned to you will review your application for basic qualifications and will match your skills and interests to a general skill area. All trainee requests are grouped into 60 generic types of assignments, for example, forestry, fisheries, construction, nursing, nutrition, science teaching. Each assignment area describes the experience or educational background needed to serve as a Peace Corps volunteer in that assignment area. If you meet these qualifications, you will be sent a list of the assignment areas for which you qualify, along with a request for you to schedule an interview.

Interviews

Once it has been determined that you meet the qualifications of a particular assignment area, you will be invited for an interview. This usually takes place within two weeks of receipt of your application. During your interview your recruiter will explore your flexibility, adaptability, social sensitivity, cultural awareness, motivation, and commitment to Peace Corps service.

Also, you will need to decide whether Peace Corps service is for you. Your recruiter will not nominate you to an assignment area without an expression of genuine commitment on your part to Peace Corps service.

In addition to your having been interviewed and determined to have the basic skills host countries want, there must be an open request for someone with your specific skills at the time you are available. If there is such an opening, your application competes with others in the recruitment office for that opening.

Nomination can be very competitive, especially for liberal arts majors.

Nomination

If you are chosen to fill the opening, you will be nominated. This means that your recruiter formally submits your name to the volunteer delivery system. It is important to emphasize that as a nominee, you are being considered, along with all other nominees in your particular assignment area, for various specific country assignments that begin training in that season.

At the time you are nominated, your recruiter may be able to tell you the geographic region for which you are being considered— for example, Africa, Asia, the Pacific—but will not be able to tell you to which specific country you may be invited.

Also remember that host countries make these requests up to 12 months before training begins. Thus they are subject to change, often at the last minute. You will know your specific country of assignment when and if you receive an invitation.

Your recruiter will notify you when you are nominated. At that time you will be given an assignment area name and number. It is also at this point that your references are contacted by mail and your application is forwarded to the Washington, D.C., evaluation division.

Shortly after you are notified of your nomination, you will receive a nomination kit, which includes a letter confirming your nomination and explaining the evaluation process, and forms that you must complete and return immediately to the evaluation division. At this time you should also contact your references and urge them to complete their reference forms as soon as possible to avoid delays.

Your Application

Once you are nominated, your application and a summary of your interview are sent to the evaluation division. You will receive a letter from the evaluation division stating that your file has been received. Your evaluator reviews your application to make sure that your qualifications match the assignment area skill requirements and checks for clarity, accuracy, and completeness.

References

Evaluators also collect and review references. It is important that your references send their forms in without delay.

Medical History

When you apply to become a volunteer, you will be asked to fill out a medical history. Check your health records so that the health conditions, treatments, and dates you report are correct. Completing this history accurately and completely allows the Peace Corps to conduct a timely evaluation of your application to be a volunteer.

This history and the subsequent physical/dental exams are extremely important. Here's why: a health condition you manage easily at home can become a serious medical problem in the countries the Peace Corps serves. Host countries do not often have U.S. levels of medical care; sites can be remote, and assignments often are physically and emotionally challenging.

When Peace Corps Medical Services is aware of all your conditions, it can do its best to find countries and living arrangements where your needs can be met. Providing incomplete or inaccurate information about your medical background can jeopardize your health once you are in service. What's more, providing false information or withholding information in any part of your application may disqualify you from consideration for service or result in separation from service.

At the next stage of the process after the history, you will receive a medical kit with instructions for completing both a physical and dental exam. You should make appointments for such exams as soon as you receive the kit. The Peace Corps will reimburse a portion but not all of costs involved. This is explained in the kit.

Legal Information

Only applicants who meet the standards of eligibility established by Congress and the Peace Corps may be invited to enter training for a volunteer assignment. If any of the following situations applies to you, your application will be put on legal hold and reviewed by the legal liaison. Further documentation on these issues will be required and the legal liaison will either clear or retire your file based on the content of those additional documents. The following circumstances do not necessarily disqualify you from Peace Corps service but require further attention and documentation: common-law marriages; serving without spouse, or divorced; dependents under 18; previous convictions; student loans (except Perkins Loans and National Direct Student Loans); financial obligations such as home mortgage payments or child support; bankruptcy; association with intelligence activity; application on file with intelligence agency; current obligations with the armed forces, National Guard, or reserve forces; impending legal proceedings involving the applicant.

Evaluation

If your references respond promptly, the evaluation process generally takes five to seven weeks. If all goes well, the evaluation division will send you a letter stating that you are qualified for Peace Corps service. Note that medical qualification is a separate process from suitability qualification. It is possible to be found suitability qualified and medically not qualified, and vice versa. Your application is then forwarded to the placement office for further consideration and matching to specific country programs.

Placement

The placement office is divided into four skill desks: agriculture, forestry, and fisheries; professional and technical trades; health; and education.

Each skill desk has two or three placement specialists who review and select applicants for specific volunteer assignments. After your application arrives at the appropriate skill desk in the placement office, it is again reviewed for suitability and technical competence, this time against country-specific criteria.

Placement specialists make the final decision to invite or not to invite a candidate to training. The process is competitive and is designed to ensure that Peace Corps volunteers have not only the technical skills needed for their assignments but also the personal qualities necessary to work successfully in specific Peace Corps assignments. They also take into consideration motivation, maturity, flexibility, and interpersonal skills.

Though you are initially nominated into a general skill area, all of your skills are taken into consideration in determining whether (and to where) you receive an invitation. Because of the competitive nature of the placement process, it can be lengthy. Your application also may be delayed due to a legal or medical hold. This phase may take anywhere from one to nine months.

If you receive an invitation, you will have ten days to respond. The invitation packet also includes a volunteer assignment description, more forms to complete (passport and visa applications), and an invitation booklet that will guide you through subsequent steps.

Training

Once you have accepted an invitation, the Peace Corps will send you the specific information you will need to prepare for training. The country desk officer will send you a packet of detailed information about your host country and a description of your training. The packet will include a recommended clothing list and a country-specific bibliography. Later you will receive instructions with details about time, date, and location of your predeparture orientation.

The travel office will send you airline tickets if you have been medically and dentally qualified, and soon you will be on your way.

The Master's International Program

The Peace Corps Master's International Program offers you the opportunity to combine graduate school with the Peace Corps experience. Through partnerships with more than 20 schools offering master's-level studies in forestry/natural resource management, agriculture, public health/nutrition, Teaching English to Speakers of Other Languages (TESOL), public policy/NGO development, business, urban planning and civil and environmental engineering, you can become a Peace Corps volunteer as partial fulfillment of your graduate degree. Most of the participating schools often grant credit at no cost for Peace Corps service.

Master's International Programs are offered in disciplines where there are shortages of skilled people who can serve as Peace Corps volunteers.

As a Master's Internationalist, you will typically complete your on-campus studies prior to entering the Peace Corps. You receive practical experience from the Peace Corps, including three months of language, and technical and cross-cultural training. Upon completion of your Peace Corps service, you return to the United States to complete any final requirements and receive your degree.

The Peace Corps does not provide scholarships to Master's International students. However, some student loans can be deferred or canceled, and all costs associated with your Peace Corps experience are covered by the Peace Corps, including transport, medical care, and living expenses. In addition the Peace Corps provides a $5,400 readjustment allowance that is paid to you at the end of your assignment. Most schools provide students with an opportunity for research or teaching assistantships, scholarships, or a tuition waiver for the cost of credits earned while in the Peace Corps.

More information is available on the Peace Corps website, peace corps.gov, or you can e-mail mastersinternational@peacecorps.gov.

United Nations Volunteers

The United Nations Volunteers program was established in 1971 by the United Nations General Assembly and is administered by the United Nations Development Program. Currently there are more than 2,500 U.N. Volunteers from around the world serving in developing countries. Of this corps of volunteers in the field, there are approximately 50 United States citizens serving in primarily two-year assignments. The United States sends about 25 U.S. citizens per year to serve as U.N. Volunteers. The majority of U.N. Volunteers—approximately 57 percent—serve in Africa, 23 percent in Asia and the Pacific, 12 percent in the Middle East and the former Soviet Union, and about 8 percent in Latin and South America.

U.N. Volunteers on the average are in their early forties and have a bachelor's degree (and often subsequent degrees), 15 to 20 years of professional experience in their field, and substantial work experience in developing countries.

U.N. Volunteers who have specialized and technical skills are recruited in fields including, but not limited to: university-level professorships in English and business; civil, electrical, and mechanical engineering; systems analysis; water and sanitation management; forestry and natural resource management; agriculture; and health. Unfortunately, candidates with generalist backgrounds are seldom accepted into the program.

United Nations Volunteers is a highly competitive program with long waiting periods. There are no guarantees of placement, and applicants are encouraged to keep other options open.

All American U.N. Volunteers are legally Peace Corps volunteers assigned to the U.N. Volunteers program. They are issued both the Peace Corps and the U.N. Volunteers oaths. They can be accompanied by up to three dependents (spouse plus two children under 18 years of age). Volunteers with dependents are more difficult to place. Some countries will request single volunteers only, because they are unable to provide suitable accommodations for families.

Married couples who apply to U.N. Volunteers and who both want to serve are almost impossible to place. It is extremely rare for two positions to become available in the same place at the same time.

Conditions of Service for U.N. Volunteers Specialists

U.N. Volunteers assignments usually last 24 months. Shorter assignments also may be authorized.

U.N. Volunteers specialists are entitled to annual leave at the rate of two and a half working days a month, which they will be required to take during their term of assignment. Such leave will need to be arranged with the supervisor and the United Nations Development Program resident representative. No payment in lieu of accrued leave may be made.

The engagement as a U.N. Volunteers specialist may be terminated by either side on six weeks' written notice. No travel costs for the specialist's spouse will be borne by the U.N. Volunteers if the volunteer resigns from his or her post before the six weeks' notice. Travel of the volunteer and up to two dependent children will be covered by the Peace Corps.

Benefits Covered by the Peace Corps

U.N. Volunteers specialists and their dependent children receive a predeparture medical examination at Peace Corps' expense. (The volunteer's acceptance is conditional on a predeparture medical clearance by both the Peace Corps and the U.N. Volunteers program.)

Travel is provided by the Peace Corps for the volunteer and up to two dependent children authorized by U.N. Volunteers to accompany the volunteer to the country of assignment. (Recognized dependent children are the specialist's own or legally adopted unmarried children up to 18 years of age.)

An amount corresponding to $200 per month of service will be paid after the completion of a volunteer's contract. Before departure from duty station, the U.N. Volunteers specialist receives one-third of the accumulated resettlement allowance. The balance is payable to the specialist at his or her home of record.

Benefits Covered by the U.N. Volunteers Program

Costs for the specialist's nonworking spouse will be covered by the U.N. Volunteers program, not by the Peace Corps. In rare cases where the duration of the assignment is for a period under the normal two years, travel costs of the spouse must be covered by the volunteer.

The monthly living allowance (MLA) ranges from $450 to $1,140 for single specialists and from $620 to $1,540 for specialists with direct dependents (spouse without gainful employment and/or minor children), depending on the costs of living at the duty station. In the case of the MLA, the dependency rate applies whether or not the dependents reside with the U.N. Volunteers specialist in the country of assignment.

The amount of the allowance may be adjusted each month (increased or decreased) according to the rate of exchange and variation in the cost-of-living level established by the U.N. for each country. Payment is normally made in the local currency, but exceptions may be authorized for certain duty stations, depending on the local living conditions.

Adequate and simply furnished accommodations, including utilities, is normally provided free of charge. If this is not possible, reimbursement of the actual rent paid will be made (up to a fixed limit). In certain countries, permanent accommodation may not be immediately available, in which case transitional arrangements will be made.

Life, health, and permanent disability are provided free of cost to each U.N. Volunteers specialist. Dependents residing with the specialist at the duty station are covered under the health insurance scheme only.

Application Procedures for U.S. Citizens

The Peace Corps is the cosponsoring agency for U.S. citizens. To apply to the U.N. program, you must complete both the United Nations Volunteers and Peace Corps applications. (See earlier in this chapter for more information on Peace Corps applications.)

You can obtain the appropriate application forms by contacting:

Peace Corps
United Nations Volunteers
1990 K Street NW
Washington, D.C. 20526
peacecorps.gov

The entire application process, from submitting the Peace Corps and U.N. Volunteers applications to being accepted onto the U.N. Volunteers roster, takes a minimum of six months. Once rostered there is no way to predict when, or if, a candidate will be considered for a post. The length of time spent on the roster will vary depending on the marketability of the candidate's skills, the number of candidates already on the roster in the same field, and the competitiveness of the candidate in his or her field. Each volunteer is placed individually as requests are received from the host countries. This individual placement system ensures that the best-qualified volunteer is selected and placed in a position that effectively utilizes his or her unique skills. As posts and country requests are continually changing according to the needs of host countries, the U.N. Volunteers cannot predict which posts will be opening, nor at what dates these posts will become available.

Training and Orientation

United Nations Volunteers candidates who have been accepted for a position receive no training and little, if any, briefing, as they are specialists in their fields and often have previous knowledge of what is required when working abroad. In some cases volunteers will be routed through Geneva for briefings on their way to post, but this is the exception, not the rule. Volunteers receive no cross-cultural orientation. They are expected to have researched their country of assignment before arrival. Once they arrive at post, the project manager or the United Nations Development Program resident representative will brief them. These briefings vary in length and depth. Many volunteers find that they are given very few guidelines with which to work.

8

Nonprofit Organizations

Nonprofit organizations are organizations that perform their activities without generating a profit. You will also sometimes hear about some of these organizations, especially if they perform large-scale public works under contract for governmental agencies as nongovernmental organizations, or NGOs. Either way, the goals and missions of these organizations encompass an extremely broad range of work, including education, health care, food relief and humanitarian aid, emergency and disaster relief, environmental concerns, political reform, and progressive social missions. No matter your skills and training and no matter your interests, no doubt there is an organization in the nonprofit arena where you could apply them.

Advantages and Disadvantages

There are pros and cons to weigh when considering any career. Here are some things to think about if you are looking at working for a nonprofit.

Satisfaction

Those who work in the nonprofit arena cite their beliefs or commitment to a particular cause or movement as their primary motivation for working in this sector. The ability to work on the front lines of important causes and make a difference in the world, and the chance to help people who might otherwise fall through the cracks of society are opportunities that are within your reach in the world of nonprofits.

Compensation

Sometimes, however, reality falls short of the dream in the area of earnings. Pay scales within nonprofits tend to be lower than comparable positions in for-profit ventures. Even professionals such as doctors and lawyers often must forgo some of their usual high salaries to work for these kinds of organizations.

Budgets

Like the paycheck issue, budgets within nonprofits are often tight. Managers within nonprofits often oversee critically important projects with less-than-sufficient funds and staff. Some managers are also called on to do fund-raising for the organization—or at least initiate contacts with likely major donors—in addition to their other responsibilities. Often a program head must secure funding from these kinds of donors before getting approval to launch new projects and programs. Although there are organizations where managers do believe they consistently have the resources, in terms of both manpower and budget, to fulfill their missions well, others do not. Job frustration in these situations can be intense.

When the world economic picture is poor, the problems in poor and developing countries are exacerbated and the need for assistance programs increases. However, these same world economic conditions can cause donors and foundations to be less generous, meaning less funding at times when need is greatest. People are more likely to be generous when times are good—when they feel they have dollars (or euros) to spare.

Also, sometimes a cause suffers negative publicity or an issue has turned lackluster in the public eye—these things, too, can mean a downturn in donor dollars. Projects can be suspended, scaled back, or even ended for reasons completely unrelated to their success or effectiveness. Conversely, though, organizations can often build success upon success. A major breakthrough—a new law or treaty that is a step forward for "the cause," for instance—can jumpstart further growth by renewing public interest and generating a real hunger for more progress. Serendipity plays a role, too. Sometimes a long, hard battle can suddenly be won due to an unexpected— or unrelated—event, such as a court case, the publication of a new book, or the death of a prominent figure in the movement.

How to Find Them

Many large nonprofits that are based in the United States, or are at least well known here, have offices in foreign countries and programs addressing international problems. Other, non–U.S.-based organizations are certainly worth your attention, too.

Jobs with these organizations can be found by using the same tools you use for finding other kinds of jobs—reading classified ads, checking websites, joining associations and attending conferences—that are specific to the kind of work you are looking for.

Read as much as possible in your chosen area: books, magazines, journals, and websites. Research the organizations you come across in your reading. Researching prominent individuals associated with a cause—reading their writings, learning what organizations they worked for and what degree programs they pursued before they came to prominence—can give you ideas, too.

Don't overlook the advantages of working first for a nonprofit in your chosen field in the United States. Although you might associate famine relief with parts of Africa and Asia, there are nonprofits that provide food relief and nutrition counseling in both the United States and Canada. The same can be said of volunteering for one of these organizations if a paid position is not available. Either way, the experience could give you a more impressive résumé and the certainty of knowing the ins and outs of your chosen field before you take a position that involves a move abroad. Also, you are more likely to build a network of important professional contacts and actually hear about positions that come open, once you are working within your chosen field.

Profile: The International Committee of the Red Cross (ICRC)

The International Committee of the Red Cross (ICRC) was founded in Geneva in the 1860s with two missions in mind: to bring relief to wounded soldiers on the battlefield and to develop international principles of cooperation for handling wounded soldiers. Previously, even volunteer doctors and nurses trying to give assistance during or after a battle were sometimes forbidden access by officers and soldiers. Doctors and nurses were not assumed to be neutral, and lacking any identifying emblem, could be easily mistaken for a civilian or enemy soldier.

Today the ICRC is both a driving force in the arena of international humanitarian law and does direct work in conflict response as well as assisting in the reuniting of families and communities that are torn apart by war. The work is often complex and sometimes even dangerous.

Staff

Much of the ICRC's work for the victims of conflict is in conjunction with national societies. The work of the ICRC is conducted by about 1,200 staff and delegates on field missions around the globe, coordinated and supported by a staff of another eight hundred people at its Geneva headquarters. All of these people work in conjunction with some nine thousand employees of national and local Red Crosses around the world.

Career Track and Qualifications

ICRC field personnel must be ready to leave for any destination at a moment's notice and be able to adapt to the sudden disruptions that sometimes result in their personal lives. By definition, duty stations are opened at times and in places chosen as a result of need—the existence of a conflict and the need for humanitarian operations as a result. To work in the unfamiliar environment of a country at war or emerging from war, the ICRC believes that skill in working as part of a team, interacting with people from a wide variety of backgrounds, and coping with stress and the difficult situations that cause it are key. It also helps when people have a true desire and interest in making intercultural contacts. The ICRC promotes motivated personnel who are at ease with the organization's humanitarian mission and share its fundamental values.

With a few exceptions, all headquarters posts are filled from within the organization, and serious candidates typically have held at least three field postings. The advantages to the organization are clear—staff members come to headquarters already thoroughly familiar with the organization's activities.

Preparing for a Career in Nonprofits

The fact is that some jobs in the nonprofits arena have well-established education and career tracks, but others do not. Even where there is an established route—say, a law degree or an M.B.A.—the advantage goes to those who have a documented emphasis in nonprofit issues—for instance, an M.B.A. with an emphasis in nonprofit marketing or nonprofit management. In addition, there are less-well-known degree programs, for instance M.A.s in public policy or public administration, which can be advantageous in preparation for a career in either international government service or in the nonprofit sector.

Development

One career path that is unique to the nonprofit arena is that of fund-raising, or development. Development is the function within a nonprofit that brings in the money that pays for the organization's programs and projects. Funds are raised in a variety of ways: through solicitations for paid memberships, by applying for grant money from foundations or government agencies, and through pay-for-service contracts for services performed.

We are all familiar with member solicitations that reach us over the phone, by direct mail, and in the form of TV commercials. Many professionals who develop media messages for nonprofits worked first as writers and designers in a variety of settings, from major advertising firms to publishing companies.

Skills

Also, don't be surprised if those with advanced degrees, like their brethren in the commercial side, seem to be on a faster track. In the areas of environmental protection or animal welfare, for instance, those who are veterinarians or who have Ph.D.s in environmental science or animal behavior may have an easier time rising to the upper levels of the organization. One reason for this is that they can be called on to wear many hats—managing projects and developing programs while at the same time conducting and publishing research in the organization's name.

However, even though you may not be a nurse or a public policy consultant, you, too, can have the deep satisfaction of a career working for a cause or issue close to your heart. Skills in demand everywhere in business are also in demand in the nonprofit sector—communications and translation, computer and systems networking, project management, human resources, finance and accounting—the full gamut.

Resources for Job Placement and Information

THE FOLLOWING LIST covers organizations, agencies, and government bodies named in this book. Contact them for information and application forms. Following these are additional helpful resources you also may wish to contact.

American Red Cross
National Headquarters
2025 E St. NW
Washington, DC 20006
redcross.org

Department of Defense
Office of Dependents Schools
2461 Eisenhower Ave.
Alexandria, VA 22331
odedodea.edu

Foreign Service
Department of State
Recruitment Division
P.O. Box 9317
Rosslyn Station
Arlington, VA 22209
state.gov

Fulbright Teacher Exchange Program
USIA
301 Fourth St. SW
Washington, DC 20547
fulbrightexchanges.org

International Schools Services
15 Roszel Rd.
P.O. Box 5910
Princeton, NJ 08543
iss.edu

National Association for Foreign Student Affairs (NAFSA)
Association of International Educators
1875 Connecticut Ave. NW, Ste. 1000
Washington, DC 20009-5728
nafsa.org

Overseas Personnel Programs
National Board of YMCAs
291 Broadway
New York, NY 10007
ymca.net

Peace Corps
1990 K St. NW
Washington, DC 20526
peacecorps.gov

Teachers of English to Speakers of Other Languages, Inc. (TESOL)
700 S. Washington St., Ste. 200
Alexandria, VA 22314
tesol.edu

U.S. Agency for International Development (AID)
International Development Intern Program
Recruitment Staff—PM/RS
Office of Human Resource Development and Management
Washington, DC 20523
usaid.gov

U.S. Army Corps of Engineers
Public Affairs Office
P.O. Box 2250
Winchester, VA 22601-1450
usace.army.mil

U.S. State Department
American-Sponsored Overseas Schools
A/OS Rm. 245 SA-29
Department of State
Washington, DC 20522-2902
state.gov

Recruitment and Placement Services

Educational Research Service (ERS)
2000 Clarendon Blvd.
Arlington, VA 22201
ers.org

Friends of World Teaching and Nursing
P.O. Box 1049
San Diego, CA 92112-1049
fowt.com

International Staffing
Boston Scientific Corporation
One Boston Scientific Pl.
Natick, MA 01760
bsci.com

Jobs in Government
P.O. Box 1436
Agoura Hills, CA 91376-1436
jobsingovernment.com

Queen's University Overseas Recruiting Fair
Placement Office
Faculty of Education
Queen's University
Kingston, ON K7L 3N6
Canada
http://educ.queensu.ca/~placment/recruiting.html

Register for International Service Education (RISE)
Institute of International Education
809 United Nations Plaza
New York, NY 10017
iie.org

U.S. Department of Education
415 Twelfth St. NW, Rm. 706
Washington, DC 20004
ed.gov
(Summer service employment for U.S. teachers abroad)

Associations and Resources for Educators

AFS International Intercultural Programs
71 W. Twenty-Third St., 17th Fl.
New York, NY 10010
afs.org

American Association for Adult and Continuing Education
(AAACE)
2102 Wilson Blvd., Ste. 925
Arlington, VA 22201
aaace.org

American Association of Intensive English Programs (AAIEP)
229 N. Thirty-Third St.
Philadelphia, PA 19014
aaiep.org

American Educational Research Association (AERA)
1230 Seventeenth St. NW
Washington, DC 20036
aera.net

America-Mideast Educational and Training Services, Inc.
AMIDEAST
1100 Seventeenth St. NW
Washington, DC 20036
amideast.org

Association of Recognised English Language Services (ARELS)
2 Ponypool Pl.
Valentine Pl.
London SEI 8QS
England
arels.org.uk

Association for Supervision and Curriculum Development (ASCD)
1703 Beauregard St.
Alexandria, VA 22311
ascd.org

Center for Applied Linguistics
4646 Fortieth St. NW
Washington, DC 20016
cal.org

Council for International Exchange of Scholars
3007 Tilden St. NW, Ste. 5L
Washington, DC 20008
cies.org

The Defense Language Institute
English Language Center
2235 Andrews Ave.
Lackland AFB, TX 78236-5514
dlielc.org

English International, Inc.
655 Sutter St., Ste. 500
San Francisco, CA 94108
english-international.com

Experiment in International Living
P.O. Box 676
Kipling Rd.
Brattleboro, VT 05302
experiment.org

General Board for Global Ministries
United Methodist Church
475 Riverside Dr.
New York, NY 10115
gbgm-umc.org

Institute of International Education
809 United Nations Plaza
New York, NY 10017
iie.org

Modern Language Association (MLA)
Ten Astor Pl.
New York, NY 10003
mla.org

National Center for Education Statistics
U.S. Department of Education
1990 K St. NW
Washington, DC 20006
http://nces.ed.gov

National Clearinghouse for Bilingual Education (NCBE)
The George Washington University
Center for the Study of Language and Education
2011 K St. NW, Ste. 260
Washington, DC 20037
ncbe.gwu.edu

National Education Association (NEA)
1201 Sixteenth St. NW
Washington, DC 20036
nea.org

School for International Training
Box 676
Brattleboro, VT 05301
sit.edu

University of Northern Iowa
Overseas Placement Service for Educators
East Gym, #113A
Cedar Falls, IA 50614-0390
uni.edu/placemnt/overseas

Appendix B

Job-Related Publications

THE FOLLOWING PUBLICATIONS advertise job openings or provide more information on opportunities working and living overseas.

Chronicle of Higher Education
Subscription Department
Chronicle of Higher Education
P.O. Box 1955
Marion, OH 43305
http://chronicle.com

EL Gazette
P.O. Box 464, Berkhamsted
Hertfordshire HP4 2UR
United Kingdom
info@elgazette.com

English Teaching Forum
USIA
301 Fourth St. SW
Washington, DC 20547
http://exchanges.state.gov/forum

The Forum
National Clearinghouse for Bilingual Education
1300 Wilson Blvd.
Rosslyn, VA 22209
http://ncbe.gwu.edu
(the newsletter of the National Clearinghouse for Bilingual
  Education)

The Guardian
Guardian Newspapers, Ltd.
164 Deansgate
Manchester M60 2RR
United Kingdom
http://jobs.guardian.co.uk

Higher Education and National Affairs
American Council on Education
One Dupont Circle
Washington, DC 20036
acenet.edu/hena

The International Educator
The International Educator's Institute
445 R W. Center St.
P.O. Box 103
West Bridgewater, MA 02379
tieonline.com

The International Employment Gazette
1525 Wade Hampton Blvd.
Greenville, SC 29609
intemployment.com

International Employment Hotline
Cantrell Corp.
P.O. Box 6170
McLean, VA 22106
internationaljobs.org/monthly.html

International Herald Tribune
181 Ave. Charles de Gaulle
92200 Neuilly
France
iht.com

International Living
Agora Publications
824 E. Baltimore St.
Baltimore, MD 21202
internationalliving.com

Living Abroad
13351-D Riverside Dr., Ste. 101
Sherman Oaks, CA 91423
livingabroad.com

Times Educational Supplement
Quadrant Subscription Services, Ltd.
Oakfield House
Perrymount Rd.
Haywards Heath
West Sussex RH 16 3DH
England
tes.co.uk

Transitions Abroad
Subscriptions Dept.
TRA, Box 3000
Denville, NJ 07834
transitionsabroad.com

Selected Employment Contacts
for Teachers

Many countries recruit teaching staff through their embassies in Washington. When writing or calling a specific country's embassy, contact the education office or cultural affairs office. You can also write to a specific country's ministry of education; the address would be available through the embassy.

Selected Employers for ESL/EFL Teachers

These organizations operate schools throughout the United States and abroad and regularly recruit teachers to fill their staffing needs.

Aspect International Language Schools
Manhattan College
Riverdale, NY 10471
aspectworld.com

ELS International
9000 Overland Ave.
Culver City, CA 92030
els.com

Inlingua
551 Fifth Ave.
New York, NY 10176
inlingua.com

U.S. Territories

Director of Education
Department of Education, American Samoa
Pago Pago, American Samoa, 96920
asg-gov.com/departments/doe.home/doe.htm

Assistant Superintendent
Personnel Department of Education
Government of Guam
Agana, Guam 96910
doe.edu.gu

Personnel Officer
Public School System
Commonwealth of the Northern Mariana Islands
P.O. Box 1370
CK Saipan, MP 96950

Secretary of Education
Department of Education
Hato Rey, Puerto Rico 00900
de.gobierno.pr

Commissioner of Education
Department of Education
Charlotte Amalie, St.Thomas Virgin Islands 00801
doe.vi

Africa

Association of International Schools in Africa
c/o International School of Kenya
P.O. Box 14103
Nairobi, Kenya
aisa.or.ke

Ivory Coast

International Community School of Abidjan
c/o U.S. Embassy, Abidjan
Department of State
Washington, DC 20520
icsa.ac.ci

Asia

East Asia Regional Council of Overseas Schools
Virginia Tech Graduate Center
2990 Telestar Ct., Rms. 314 and 315
Falls Church, VA 22042
earcos.org

China

Education Division
Embassy of the People's Republic of China
2300 Connecticut Ave. NW
Washington, DC 20008
china-embassy.org/eng

China Teaching Program
Western Washington University
Old Main 530
Bellingham, WA 98225-9047
ac.wwu.edu/~ctp

CIEE, U.S.-China Educator Exchange
Professional Programs
205 E. Forty-Second St.
New York, NY 10017
ciee.org

International School of Beijing
10 An Hua St., Shunyi District
Beijing 101300
The People's Republic of China
isb.bj.edu.cn

Hong Kong

General Secretary's Office
City University of Hong Kong
83 Tat Chee Ave.
Kowloon, Hong Kong
cityu.edu.hk

Japan

JALT: The Japan Association of Language Teachers
Shamboru Dai-2 Kawasaki #305
1-3-17 Kalzuka, Kawasaki-ku
Kawasaki, 210
Japan
jalt.org

The Japan Exchange and Teaching Program
Embassy of Japan
Office of JET Program
2520 Massachusetts Ave. NW
Washington, DC 20008
jetprogramme.org

AEON Intercultural Corporation
1960 E. Grand Ave., #550
El Segundo, CA 90245
aeonet.com

Berlitz Schools of Languages in Japan
Kowa Bldg. No. 15F, 11-41 Alaska 1-chrome
Minato-ku, Tokyo 107
Japan
http://careers.berlitz.com

Korea (South)

The Dong-A School Foundation
226-2 Jayang-dong
Dong-ku, Daejeon 300-100
Korea
http://english.donga.ac.kr

Singapore

Director, Personnel Department
National University of Singapore
10 Kent Ridge Crescent
Singapore 0511
nus.edu.sg

Taiwan

KOJEN English Language Schools
6F, #9, La. 90
Sung Chiang Rd.
Taipei, Taiwan, ROC
kojenenglish.com

Thailand

Ruamrudee International School
123/15 Ruamrudee La.
Ploenchit Rd., Praturnwan
Bangkok 10330, Thailand
rism.ac.th

Western Europe

European Council of International Schools
18 Lavant St.
Petersfield, Hampshire GU32 3EW
England
ecis.org

Mediterranean Association of International Schools
c/o American School of Madrid
Apartado 80
28080 Madrid
Spain
mais-web.org

Denmark

Copenhagen International Junior School
Hellerupvej 22-26, 2900
Hellerup, Denmark
cis-edu.dk

France

International School of Paris
6 rue Beethoven
75016 Paris
France
isparis.edu

Spain

American School of Barcelona
Calle Jaume Balmes, 7
08950, Esplugues de LLobregat
Spain
a-s-b.com/intro.htm

English International College School
Urb. Ricmar
Crtr. de Cádiz-Málaga Km. 189,5
Marbella, Málaga
España
eic.edu

Eastern Europe

Central and Eastern European Schools Association
c/o Office of Overseas Schools
U.S. Department of State
Rm. 245 SA 29
Washington, DC 20522-2902
ceesa.org

Bulgaria

Anglo-American School
Department of State
5740 Sofia Pl.
Washington, DC 20521-5740
ecis.org/sofia

Middle East

Most universities in the Middle East, especially in the Persian Gulf countries, operate a language center for incoming students.

Near East South Asia Council for Overseas Schools
c/o The American Colleges of Greece
P.O. Box 600 18
153 10 Aghia, Paraskevi
Athens, Greece
nesacenter.org

Jewish Agency for Israel
515 Park Ave.
New York, NY 10022
jafi.org.il

Bahrain

Embassy of the State of Bahrain
3502 International Dr. NW
Washington, DC 20008
bahrainembassy.org

University of Bahrain
P.O. Box 32038
State of Bahrain
uob.bh

Egypt

Senior Program Officer
The Binational Fulbright Commission
1081 Cornich El Nil St.
Garden City, Cairo
Egypt
fulbright-egypt.org

The American University in Cairo
P.O. Box 2511
113 Sharia Kasr El Aini
Cairo, Egypt
or
420 Fifth Ave.
New York, NY 10018-2729
aucegypt.edu

Cairo American College
P.O. Box 39
Maadi 11431
Cairo, Egypt
cacegypt.org

Kuwait

Embassy of the State of Kuwait
2940 Tilden St. NW
Washington, DC 20008
kuwait-info.org

Morocco

Casablanca American School Administrative Officer
Route de la Mecque
Lotissement Ougoug
Quartier Californie
20150 Casablanca
Morocco
cas.ac.ma

Oman

Embassy of the Sultanate of Oman
2535 Belmont Rd. NW
Washington, DC 20008

Director, Language Centre
P.O. Box 50
Muscat 123
Sultanate of Oman
squ.edu.om

The American-British Academy
P.O. Box 372, PC 115
Medinat Al Sultan Qaboos
Muscat
Sultanate of Oman
aba-oman.com

Qatar

Embassy of the State of Qatar
4200 Wisconsin Ave. NW, Ste. 200
Washington, DC 20016

Academic Staff Recruitment Committee
University of Qatar
P.O. Box 2713
Doha, Qatar
qu.edu.qa/home

Saudi Arabia

There are numerous colleges, universities, technical and vocational schools, as well as international schools throughout Saudi Arabia. Private companies also frequently hire teachers. For a complete list of schools, contact the Saudi Education Mission. Private companies that advertise their openings that can be located in directories of overseas businesses. A few are included here.

Embassy of Saudi Arabia
601 New Hampshire Ave. NW
Washington, DC 20037
saudiembassy.net

King Saud University
College of Arts
P.O. Box 2456
Riyadh, 11451
Saudi Arabia

King Abdul Aziz University
P.O. Box 80200
Jeddah 21589
Saudi Arabia
kaau.edu.sa

The Institute of Public Administration
Riyadh 11141
Saudi Arabia
ipa.edu.sa/eng/eng100.asp

Dean of Faculty and Personnel Affairs
King Fahd University of Petroleum Minerals
Dhahran 31261
Saudi Arabia
kfupm.edu.sa

ARAMCO
P.O. Box 4530
Houston, TX 77210
saudiaramco.com

ARAMCO, or the Arabian American Oil company, hires qualified
teachers for its site in Dhahran, Saudi Arabia.

Syria

Damascus Community School
Department of State
6110 Damascus Pl.-DCS
Washington, DC 20521-6110

Al Mahdi Bin Baraka St.
Abu Rumaneh
Damascus, Syria
dcssyria.org

United Arab Emirates

Embassy of the United Arab Emirates
1010 Wisconsin Ave. NW, Ste. 700
Washington, DC 20007
uaeembassy.org

Higher Colleges of Technology
P.O. Box 47025
Al Masaood Tower, 13th Fl.
Abu Dhabi, United Arab Emirates
hct.ac.ae

The United Arab Emirates University, Al Ain
P.O. Box 15551, Al-Ain
United Arab Emirates
or
Embassy of the United Arab Emirates
Cultural Division
UAE University Office
3522 International Ct. NW, Ste. 202
P.O. Box 39305
Washington, DC 20008
uaeu.ac.ae

Yemen

Sana'a Turkish School
Box 18148
Sana'a, Yemen
tisyemen.org

Yemen American Language Institute (YALI)
P.O. Box 1088
Sana'a, Yemen
yali.org.ye

Central America

Association of American Schools of Central America, Colombia,
    Caribbean, and Mexico
c/o U.S. Embassy Quito
Unit 5372, Box 004
APO AA 34039-3420
Quito, Ecuador
tri-association.org

Network of Educators in Central America (NECA)
1118 Twenty-Second St. NW
Washington, DC 20037

South America

Association of American Schools in South America, Inc.
14750 NW Seventy-Seventh Ct., Ste. 210
Miami Lakes, FL 33016
aassa.com

Inter-Regional Center for Curriculum and Materials Development
Apartado Aereo 3250
Barranquilla, Colombia

Brazil

American School of Brasilia
SGAS 605
Bloco E
Lotes 34/37
70200-650 Brasilia
DF
Brazil
eabdf.br

Chile

Thomas Jefferson American School
Casilla 6050 Correo 5
Concepcion, Chile
tjeffersonschool.cl

Colombia

Centro Colombo Americano
Cra. 45 (El Palo)
No. 53
24 A.A.
8734 Medellin
Colombia
colomboworld.com

Recommended Reading

Bender, Elaine, et al. *Arco American Foreign Service Officer Exam*, 3rd ed. Lawrenceville, N.J.: Arco Publishing, 2001.

Carland, Maria Pinto, and Lisa A. Gihring. *Careers in International Affairs*. Washington, D.C.: Georgetown University Press, 2003.

Dikel, Margaret Riley, and Frances E. Roehm. *The Guide to Internet Job Searching*. Chicago: VGM Career Books, 2004.

Griffith, Susan. *Teaching English Abroad*, 6th ed. Guilford, Conn.: Globe Pequot Press, 2002.

Heiter, Celeste. Ganbatte *Means Go for It! Or How to Become an English Teacher in Japan*. San Francisco: ThingsAsian Press, 2002.

Krannich, Ronald L., and Wendy S. Enelow. *Best Résumés and CVs for International Jobs: Your Passport to the Global Job Market*. Manassas Park, Va.: Impact Publications, 2002.

Krannich, Ronald L., and Caryl Rae Krannich. *The Directory of Websites for International Jobs.* Manassas Park, Va.: Impact Publications, 2002.

Leonard, Barry, ed. *Overseas Employment Opportunities for Educators: Department of Defense Dependents Schools.* Chicago: DIANE Publishing Company, 2000.

Linderman, Patricia. *Realities of Foreign Service Life.* Writers Club Press, 2002.

Mohamed, Jeff. *Teaching Overseas: A Job Guide for Americans and Canadians,* 3rd ed. English International Inc., 2003.

Nelson, Janice. *Handbook for Teaching English in Mexico and Central America.* Writers Club Press, 2000.

O'Sullivan, Jerry. *Teaching English in Japan,* 2d ed. New York: McGraw-Hill, 1995.

Sargent, Porter. *Schools Abroad of Interest to Americans,* 9th ed. Boston: Porter Sargent Pub., 1999.

Thompson, Mary Anne. *The Global Résumé and CV Guide.* Hoboken, N.J.: John Wiley and Sons, 2000.

A number of publishers put out in-depth travel guides to various countries and regions in the world. Although not generally a source for jobs, these guides provide important information on living conditions. Check your newsstand or bookstores for appropriate editions.

About the Author

A FULL-TIME writer of career books, Blythe Camenson's main concern is helping job seekers make educated choices. She firmly believes that with enough information, readers can find long-term, satisfying careers. To that end, she researches traditional as well as unusual occupations, talking to a variety of professionals about what their jobs are really like. In all of her books she includes first-hand accounts from people who can reveal what to expect in each occupation.

Blythe Camenson was educated in Boston, earning her B.A. in English and psychology from the University of Massachusetts and her M.Ed. in counseling from Northeastern University.